Short Bike Rides

in and around

New York City

Phil and Wendy Harrington

An East Woods Book

The Globe Pequot Press

Old Saybrook, Connecticut

To our beloved daughter, Helen

Short Bike Rides is a trademark of The Globe Pequot Press, Inc.

Library of Congress Cataloging-in-Publication Data

Harrington, Phil.
  Short bike rides in and around New York City / by Phil and Wendy
  Harrington. — 1st ed.
      p.   cm.
  "An East Woods book."
  Includes bibliographical references.
  ISBN 1-56440-026-3
  1. Bicycle touring—New York Metropolitan Area—Guide-books.
  2. New York Metropolitan Area—Description and travel—Guide-books.
  I. Harrington, Wendy. II. Title.
GV1045.5.N72N494 1992
796.6'4'097472—dc20

91-44665
CIP

♻ This text is printed on recycled paper.

Manufactured in the United States of America
First Edition/Second Printing

Acknowledgments

One of the most rewarding aspects of researching and writing this book has been the many helpful people we have dealt with along the way. Every agency that we contacted gladly provided information and details. Were it not for their help, the quality of the book you hold would have suffered greatly.

Though we cannot possibly name everyone who has aided us throughout the two years it took to assemble this work, we would like to single out a few folks who have been especially helpful:

Elizabeth Fenton, Darien Historical Society
Eric Hilton
Pamela Hurst, Rockland Economic Development Corporation
Clif Kranish, New York Cycle Club
Anne McClellan, Neighborhood Open Space Coalition
Carol Ortner, Alley Pond Environmental Center
Joseph Paccione
Gordon Rabeler, Rockland Economic Development Corporation
Karen Sposato, Westchester County Public Information Office

To them, and to everyone who contributed to this work in one way or another, we give our heartfelt thanks.

About the Authors

Phil Harrington is an engineer at Brookhaven National Laboratories in Upton, New York, as well as a freelance writer. Over the past two decades he has biked tens of thousands of miles in and around New York City, including several "century" (100-mile) tours and other annual cycling events. He is the author of *Touring the Universe Through Binoculars* and *Star Ware*, both published by John Wiley and Sons, and is co-author of Globe Pequot's *Astronomy for All Ages*. He has written numerous articles for leading astronomical periodicals.

Wendy Harrington is former assistant director of nursing with the Kings Park Psychiatric Center in Kings Park, New York, as well as an aspiring author of children's books. She is a member of both Who's Who in American Nursing and Sigma Alpha Tau (nursing's national honor society). She describes herself as a casual weekend cyclist who prefers to "stop and smell the roses" rather than race past the sights.

Together with their daughter, Helen, the Harringtons spend many weekends touring the New York tristate area on two wheels.

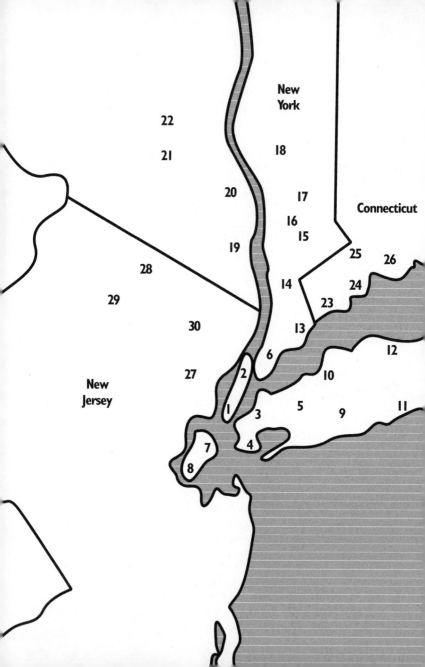

Contents

Connecticut

New Jersey

Introduction

Most people wouldn't think of using the words *bicycling* and *New York City* in the same sentence. After all, New York has the reputation of being one huge traffic snarl complicated by potholes, irate cabbies, double-parked cars, and death-defying drivers darting about. While this may be true some of the time in some parts of the city, at other times, and in other parts, New York can take on the serenity of a small town. Indeed, the city offers a wide and varied environment for the bike rider. Nowhere else in the world can two such divergent themes be so successfully combined as in New York City. The urban cyclist just has to be a little clever.

In this book we take you, the reader and cyclist, on a tour of the five boroughs of New York City by bike. City cycling is like nothing you have ever experienced before! It is both exhilarating and relaxing at the same time—a true dichotomy. You will enjoy it.

Likewise, the countryside around New York City offers a tremendous range of settings for the cyclist. Within an hour's drive you will find everything from long, flat beachfront expanses that appeal to the casual rider, to hilly terrain that will test the most seasoned biker. Whether you are an urbanite seeking escape or a suburbanite seeking adventure, you will find what you are looking for here.

Be it urban, suburban, or rural, each route has been chosen on the basis of several criteria, such as the amount of traffic, road-surface quality, terrain, scenic beauty, historical significance, and general interest. Some of the rides are full loops, while others require you to backtrack over the same roads home. We hope you will get a chance to try them all.

We have provided directions to the beginning of each ride from a nearby major highway. Of course, it is not always practical or possible for all readers to get to the starting points by automobile. With this in mind, we have listed the closest railroad station as well. But remember, the Metropolitan Transportation Authority (which governs the Long Island Railroad and Metro North) allows bicycles on off-peak trains only. For further information about obtaining the required permit, contact the Metropolitan Transportation Authority at (212) 878–7000, or your nearest railroad station. Bicycles are *not* currently permitted on city subways or buses or on New Jersey Transit trains.

As you browse through these thirty rides, you will notice that many can be connected to form longer journeys. In some cases two rides share some common roads, while others may be linked by short connectors. Still others may be teamed up with rides from other books in the Globe Pequot Short Bike Rides series.

We have tried to make the accompanying maps as complete and informative as possible. Along with street names and attractions, they include the suggested direction of travel, location of larger hills ("+" for uphill, "–" for downhill), and possible shortcuts.

Here are a few general tips and suggestions for all cyclists:

Bikes. Nowadays most cyclists prefer to use multispeed bicycles. They come in a variety of shapes and sizes, but the perennial favorite seems to be the "racing-style" machine. These bikes are characterized by their light weight, downturned handlebars, narrow saddles, and skinny tires.

Actually, labeling all bikes of this genre as "racers" is a bit of a misnomer. Most should be labeled either "touring" bikes or "road" bikes. Regardless of the name, this style of bicycle is excellent for touring most suburban and country thoroughfares.

A growing segment of the bicycling population is turning toward a completely different type of bicycle: the mountain bike or all-terrain bicycle (ATB for short). The ATB features thick, knobby tires, a reinforced frame, straight handlebars, and a cushioned saddle. Most are equipped with advanced hand-brake systems and 10- to 21-speed gearing. While the use of touring/road/racing bikes should be confined to paved and hard-packed dirt roads, mountain bikes are sturdy enough to blaze their own trails. The ruggedness of all-terrain bikes accounts for their popularity among city dwellers.

A third type whose popularity is also growing fast is the "hybrid." As the name implies, this bicycle takes features from both the "racer" (light weight, thin tires) and the "ATB" (upright handlebars, cushiony seat, and the shape of the frame) and combines them into one package. Many cyclists believe that hybrids are the best all-around bikes.

Helmets. The single most important accessory you can buy is a cycling helmet. Not convinced? Once we were riding along a quiet road on Long Island when, while going down a steep hill and around a sharp curve, Phil met a pothole about 3 feet wide and 9 inches deep. The pothole won the fight and Phil went flying, only to meet the road head-on! Were it not for his helmet, he surely would have suffered a concussion or skull fracture. (He ended up with only minor whiplash, though his left leg was a bit mangled!) 'Nuff said— get a helmet and make sure it meets either ANSI or Snell criteria (two testing organizations).

Locks. Your bicycle is a hot property in and around New York City, and there are those who want to take it from you. While there is no absolute way to prevent theft, the bicycling advocate association Transportation Alternatives recommends cross-locking bikes with two kinds of locks. One should be a hardened steel chain with a hardened lock; the other a U-lock, Cobra lock, or Disk lock. It is also a good idea to take your front wheel with you. For the outer boroughs and suburbs, a medium-weight cable or U-lock is usually sufficient. Secure both wheels and the frame to something that will prevent the thief from slipping the lock and bike over it (a permanent bike rack, street sign, or twin parking meter are best). U-locks can be slipped over smaller, single parking meters.

Safety. The law of the land requires cyclists to follow all rules applicable to cars. These include obeying all traffic lights and signs, using hand signals when turning, and riding on the right-hand side of the road (with traffic, not against it).

In this day and age, violent crime can happen anywhere. That's why we recommend that you always ride with a friend—there is safety in numbers. Also, be sure to bring along spare parts and tools in case an emergency repair is needed. Here's a list of the most commonly needed items:

Spare tube (bring two)
Tire-repair kit (patch kit, tire irons, etc.)
Hand pump
Air-pressure gauge
Adjustable wrench
Twin-blade reversible screwdriver
First-aid kit

Sure, they add some weight but we would rather carry a few extra pounds than be left stranded in the middle of nowhere.

Every resident of the New York City tristate area is well aware that road conditions are constantly changing. A smooth, pleasant road today can be transformed into a dug-up construction site tomorrow. That cannot be helped or anticipated. If you have suggestions or comments on how the routes can be modified or improved, however, we eagerly welcome your thoughts. Jot them down and send them to us in care of Globe Pequot Press, P.O. Box 833 Old Saybrook, Connecticut 06475. All suggestions will be considered for future editions. We will attempt to acknowledge all correspondence, but in case we miss yours, thanks in advance.

Happy, safe cycling!

Manhattan
The Battery to the Village

Mileage:	5
Approximate pedaling time:	1 hour
Terrain:	Flat
Traffic:	Disastrous on weekdays but light on both weekend and holiday mornings.
Things to see:	Battery Park, Lower New York Harbor (including the Statue of Liberty), Castle Clinton National Monument, Eisenhower War Memorial, American Stock Exchange, World Trade Center, Tribeca, Soho, Greenwich Village, Washington Square Park, New York University, City Hall, Trinity Episcopal Church, New York Stock Exchange, Federal Hall National Memorial, Fraunces Tavern

Although this is one of the nation's most hectic areas five days a week, the concrete canyons of Manhattan's financial district take on the eerie emptiness of a ghost town on weekend and holiday mornings. It is at those times that the city's hustle and bustle give way to the quiet serenity of a morning bike ride.

Our trip around lower Manhattan starts in **Battery Park** at the island's southern tip. The site of a fort built in 1624 by the city's first Dutch settlers, the Battery offers commanding views of the lower **New York Harbor** and the **Statue of Liberty**. The park itself has many paved sidewalks for a slow (and cautious) tour. Within Battery Park is the **Castle Clinton National Monument**. Built in 1811, it served as army headquarters during the War of 1812 and as a defense outpost

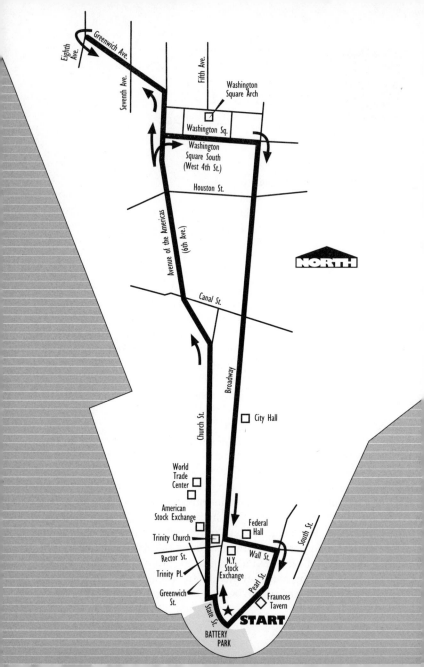

DIREC-TIONS at a glance

0.0 Begin at corner of State and Pearl streets, across from Battery Park.

0.1 Left on Battery Place, then left on Greenwich Street.

0.3 Veer right onto Trinity Place, which changes names to Church Street at the World Trade Center.

1.2 Left onto the Avenue of the Americas (6th Avenue).

2.2 Right onto Washington Square South (West 4th Street).

2.6 Right at first traffic light after Washington Square Park onto Broadway.

4.3 Left across from Trinity Church onto Wall Street.

4.5 Bear right onto Pearl Street. Take Pearl Street to State Street and Battery Park.

to guard the port of New York. Also found within Battery Park is the **Eisenhower War Memorial,** which pays homage to the thousands of U.S. soldiers who died overseas during World War II.

The ride begins at the park's northern perimeter. Head north on Greenwich Street, then veer right onto Trinity Place. About 0.25 mile along you will pass 86 Trinity Place, home of the **American Stock Exchange.** North of this point Trinity Place changes names to Church Street.

As you pass the intersection of Church and Liberty streets, you will be riding in the shadow of the **World Trade Center,** a sixteen-acre office and plaza complex completed in 1970. Standing next to the twin 110-story towers while straddling a bicycle can certainly make one feel insignificant! If you have never walked through the Trade Center plaza, take the time to do so—but first find a place to lock your bike up securely. Inside are many renowned retail stores and eateries. If time permits, take the elevator up, up, up to the 107th-floor indoor observation deck or the 110th-floor open promenade. The panoramic view from either floor is truly breathtaking.

Back down on the ground, press northward on Church Street,

leaving the financial district behind. The route now enters **Tribeca** (named for the *Tri*angle *Be*low *Ca*nal Street) and then **Soho** (the area *So*uth of *Ho*uston Street), two trendy residential areas.

Veer left onto the Avenue of the Americas (6th Avenue). At Washington Square South (West 4th Street) turn right. You are now in the heart of **Greenwich Village,** well known for its bookstores, boutiques, and art galleries. A short side trip along Greenwich Avenue will reveal many small handicraft, clothing, and jewelry shops (try not to buy too much—remember the trip home).

Pedaling eastward along Washington Square South, the route traverses the southern perimeter of **Washington Square Park.** At the head of the square stands the mighty Washington Arch, designed by Stanford White. The park is an ongoing three-season festival, with art shows and informal folk and jazz concerts found here throughout the spring, summer, and fall. Surrounding the park is the campus of **New York University.**

Continue east of Washington Square Park to the first traffic light; turn right onto Broadway. As you make your way southward along the lower end of the "Great White Way," you will pass **City Hall** nestled in a pleasant park on the corner of Broadway and Chambers Street.

Farther down Broadway, at the corner of Rector Street, lies **Trinity Episcopal Church.** The original structure on this site was completed by early settlers in 1697 and later served as the first home of King's College in the mid-1700s. (King's College later moved uptown and changed its name to Columbia University.) The present structure was constructed in 1846. Allow enough time to visit the church's museum and to take one of the tours offered weekdays at 2 P.M. As you walk around the churchyard, look for the headstones of Alexander Hamilton and Robert Fulton, both buried out back.

Leaving the churchyard, cross Broadway and turn left onto Wall Street, home of the **New York Stock Exchange.** The Stock Exchange is closed on weekends and holidays but open on regular business days with free tours and a visitor's gallery. If you are planning a visit, we suggest that you do so on foot; this is no place for a bicycle!

Farther down Wall Street pause at the **Federal Hall National Memorial.** Federal Hall served as both the site of Washington's inauguration on April 30, 1789, and the nation's Capitol until August 1790. Although the present building is just over 100 years old, it houses the original brown slab upon which Washington stood to take his oath of office.

As you approach the east end of Wall Street, you have a choice to make. To return to Battery Park, turn right onto Pearl Street. If you wish, instead, to link up with Ride #3 (visiting the South Street Seaport, the Brooklyn Bridge, and Brooklyn Heights), continue one block farther to South Street and bear left.

The last stop before the ride's end is at **Fraunces Tavern** at 54 Pearl Street. This was the 1783 site of Washington's farewell to the officers of the Continental Army, as well as the first home of the United States War Department. Today, Fraunces Tavern is a restored museum and restaurant.

From Fraunces Tavern continue along Pearl Street to State Street. There, adjacent to the Staten Island Ferry terminal, is Battery Park, your starting point.

For Further Information

Castle Clinton National Monument (212) 344–7220
World Trade Center Visitors' Information (212) 466–7397
Trinity Episcopal Church (212) 602–0800
New York Stock Exchange (212) 623–5167
Federal Hall National Memorial (212) 264–4367
Fraunces Tavern (212) 425–1776

Getting There

On weekends parking is available along many of the side streets near Battery Park, but pay close attention to any restrictions. There are also several parking lots and garages available. If you live in Brooklyn, Queens, Staten Island, or New Jersey, you might prefer to leave your car on Staten Island and take the ferry to Manhattan.

Manhattan
Central Park

Mileage:	7
Approximate pedaling time:	1 hour
Terrain:	Hilly in spots
Traffic:	Light to nil
Things to see:	Tavern on the Green, Sheep Meadow, the Pond, Wollman Memorial Rink, Gotham Miniature Golf Course, the Carousel, the Dairy, Central Park Zoo, Children's Zoo, the Mall, the Bandshell, Bethesda Fountain, the Lake, Cleopatra's Needle, the Great Lawn, the Metropolitan Museum of Art, the Reservoir, Strawberry Fields

If you are like us, then you are probably silently envious of professional racing cyclists who actually get paid to pedal. Though you may not be ready to compete against Greg LeMond, you can ride in his shadow as you cycle this circuit of Central Park, which was used in the 1990 Tour de Trump bicycle race (subsequently reincarnated as the Tour DuPont). Happily, the park roads are closed to automobiles from 10 A.M. to 3 P.M. on weekdays and all day Saturday and Sunday, with extended hours during the summer. Just watch out for pedestrians and other cyclists!

Begin where the racers did, at the West 67th Street entrance to the park. There, on the right, is the world-famous restaurant, **Tavern on the Green.** No doubt some of the patrons would be surprised to learn that the restaurant was originally built to house sheep. In fact, sheep called Central Park home as recently as 1930. The large open field bordering the road to the left is still referred to as **Sheep Meadow.**

7

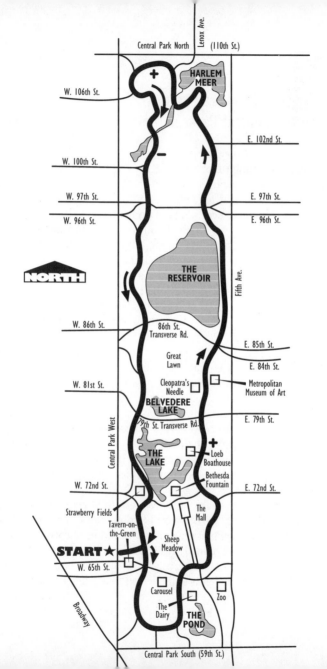

NORTH

Lenox Ave.

Central Park North   (110th St.)

HARLEM
MEER

W. 106th St.

+

E. 102nd St.

W. 100th St.

−

W. 97th St.   E. 97th St.

W. 96th St.   E. 96th St.

THE
RESERVOIR

Fifth Ave.

W. 86th St.   86th St.
Transverse Rd.

Great
Lawn

E. 85th St.

E. 84th St.

Cleopatra's
Needle

Metropolitan
Museum of Art

W. 81st St.

BELVEDERE
LAKE

79th St. Transverse Rd.   E. 79th St.

Central Park West

THE LAKE

+
Loeb
Boathouse

Bethesda
Fountain

W. 72nd St.   E. 72nd St.

Strawberry Fields

Tavern-on-
the-Green

The
Mall

START ★

Sheep
Meadow

W. 65th St.

Broadway

Carousel

The
Dairy

Zoo

THE
POND

Central Park South (59th St.)

**DIREC-
TIONS**
at a glance

No specific directions are needed for this ride.
Enter the park at West 67th Street (or at one of its
many other entrances) and proceed to the right
along West (or East) Drive on the designated bike
lane.

Turn right onto West Drive and proceed southward. The road
soon veers to the left to become East Drive, heading uptown. Beyond
the trees on the right is a horseshoe-shaped body of water simply
called the **Pond**. It's a lovely place to pause and soak up a bit of nature. Just beyond the Pond is **Wollman Memorial Rink**. From April
to October the rink is outfitted for roller skating, while ice skaters
enjoy the facility during the winter months. Next to the rink is the
Gotham Miniature Golf Course. Created under the auspices of Don-
ald Trump, the course features a creative setting around scale models
of city landmarks. The rink and golf course are open daily with nominal fees for players.

As you approach the 65th Street overpass, don't be surprised if
you hear carousel music coming from the left. The **Carousel** was
built in 1908 for Coney Island and later moved to Central Park. Its
fifty-eight hand-carved horses continue to delight today's children
just as they did their great-grandparents almost a century ago.

Across East Drive from the Carousel, look for the **Dairy**, a dark-
brown building set among a thicket of trees. Dating back to a time
when cows grazed nearby, the Dairy is now home to the park's visitors' center. Inside you will find a wide variety of exhibits, maps, and
brochures describing the park's many programs. Be sure to stop in.

The **Central Park Zoo** is another park attraction that is enjoying a
rebirth after major renovation. Centrally located in the zoo is the sea-
lion pool. It is easy to become entranced while watching these playful
creatures swim about. Surrounding the pool are exhibit halls highlighting different climates. These range from a frigid arctic setting to a
tropical rain forest. Nearby, the **Children's Zoo** makes a delightful
stop for younger cyclists.

Just past the zoo on the left is a 1,212-foot-long promenade called the **Mall.** Its wide walkway is lined with statues of famous authors, including Shakespeare and Sir Walter Scott, and shaded by two rows of noble elm trees. At the north end of the Mall stands the **Bandshell**, where concerts and performances are held nearly every night during the summer months. Farther along, at the 72nd Street transverse, is the **Bethesda Fountain.** The fountain's link to its biblical namesake, the Bethesda Pool, is made immediately apparent by the statue of an angel in its center.

From the fountain you have a magnificent view of the **Lake.** The Loeb Boathouse, on the Lake's eastern shore, rents bicycles to visitors who want to join in the fun of touring Central Park by pedal power. The boathouse also rents rowboats for use on the Lake. You'll find a restaurant and a snack bar there as well.

As you cross 79th Street, look on the left for **Cleopatra's Needle**, an Egyptian obelisk made of pink granite. This unique gift was presented to New York City in 1881 by the khedive of Egypt. Beyond the obelisk lies the **Great Lawn,** a pleasant spot to picnic or rest.

Across the way on the right is the **Metropolitan Museum of Art.** Its collection of more than three million works of art makes this the largest art museum in the Western Hemisphere. The museum is open Tuesdays through Sundays but is closed on most holidays. Bicycle parking is available in the underground garage.

In many ways Central Park itself is a fine work of art. Although it has the appearance of a natural landscape, every square inch was meticulously planned and created by Frederick Law Olmsted and Calvert Vaux in the mid-nineteenth century. Before construction began in 1858, the area was a swampy dumping ground described by the *New York Post* as a "waste land, ugly and repulsive." Sixteen years and $14 million later, Olmsted and Vaux had created an 840-acre park that is enjoyed by more than three million people annually.

East Drive veers to the right as it passes the **Reservoir.** Actually, this body of water no longer serves as a functional reservoir since the city gets most of its drinking water from a series of large reservoirs upstate. If you wish, you may walk your bike along the jogging path and bridle path surrounding the reservoir (but please refrain from riding on these trails).

Continue beyond the waters of the Harlem Meer (though *Webster's Unabridged Dictionary* does not define what a "meer" is, it looks like a pond to us) to begin the journey back south. Up to this point the park road has been either flat or downhill, but now it is time to pay the piper. As you loop past the 105th Street exits, you begin the climb up the park's aptly named "Great Hill." Thankfully, the ascent does not last terribly long before the road begins to descend once again.

Opposite the park's West 72nd Street entrance is **Strawberry Fields**. More than 160 species of trees, shrubs, and flowers from 150 countries follow the curved footpaths as they ascend a small hill. Named for the well-known song by the Beatles, Strawberry Fields is a living monument to the late John Lennon, who lived at 72nd Street and Central Park West.

The ride concludes in five blocks back at the West 67th Street park entrance. Care to take another lap?

For Further Information

Tavern on the Green (212) 873–3200
Wollman Memorial Rink (212) 517–4800
The Dairy (212) 397–3156
Central Park Carousel (212) 879–0244
Loeb Boathouse (212) 288–7281
Metropolitan Museum of Art (212) 535–7710

Getting There

Central Park is bounded on the south by 59th Street, on the east by Fifth Avenue, on the north by 110th Street, and on the west by Central Park West. Parking is at a premium, though spaces may be found on adjacent streets (most readily on weekend mornings). Be sure to note the alternate-side-of-the-street parking rules before leaving. For suburbanites, take the train to Grand Central or Penn station, then proceed northward along one of the avenues to the park.

Manhattan/Brooklyn
A Two-Borough Tour

Mileage:	8
Approximate pedaling time:	1 hour
Terrain:	Flat
Traffic:	Moderate to heavy
Things to see:	South Street Seaport, St. Paul's Chapel, Brooklyn Bridge, Brooklyn Heights, Brooklyn Historical Society

Step back in time to the Manhattan of the nineteenth century. Far down on the Lower East Side, life centers around the city's seaport, the heart of worldwide trade and commerce. Here, ships heavily laden with all sorts of cargo regularly sail in and out of port, bound for all corners of the globe.

Across the East River, Brooklyn is a completely different world. Tree-lined cobblestoned streets flanked by residences create a sense of tranquility, in sharp contrast to the hectic pace of the big city.

Return to today for a tour of these two diverse neighborhoods. Start at the famed **South Street Seaport**, near the corner of South and Fulton streets. One hundred years ago all goods shipped into and out of New York passed through the seaport. Abandoned shortly after the turn of the century when shipping moved to piers in the Hudson River, the seaport was resurrected in the 1960s as historic preservation efforts got underway.

Between South and Water streets, Fulton Street was converted into a pedestrian mall lined with shops and restaurants. Just up Fulton on the right is the Fulton Market Building, the fourth market to be built on this site since 1822. It houses a wide variety of food and souvenir outlets. Do you smell fish? Probably, since the South Street side of the

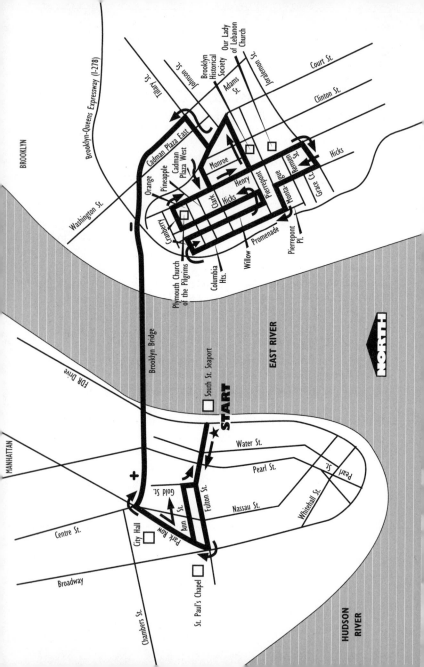

DIRECTIONS at a glance

0.0	Head west on Fulton Street from South Street.
0.5	Right onto Broadway.
0.6	Right onto Park Row.
0.7	Left onto Centre Street.
0.8	Follow signs toward Brooklyn Bridge bicycle/pedestrian path.

2.2 Leaving bridge, turn right onto Tillary Street.
2.3 Right onto Cadman Plaza West.
2.4 Left onto Clark Street.
2.5 Left onto Henry Street.
2.8 Right onto Joralemon Street.
2.9 Right onto Hicks Street.
3.1 Left onto Montague Street.
3.2 Right onto Pierrepont Place.
3.3 Left onto Columbia Heights.
3.6 Right onto Cranberry Street.
3.7 Right onto Willow Street.
4.0 Left onto Pierrepont Street.
4.1 Left onto Hicks Street.
4.4 Right onto Cranberry Street.
4.5 Right onto Henry Street.
4.8 Left onto Pierrepont Street.
5.0 Left onto Cadman Plaza West.
5.1 Right onto Tillary Street.
5.2 Left onto Brooklyn Bridge bikeway.
6.6 Left onto Park Row.
6.9 Left onto Ann Street.
7.1 Right onto Gold Street.
7.2 Left onto Fulton Street.
7.5 Back at Fulton and South streets.

building is home to the Fulton Fish Market. The fish is fresh daily; the market has been operating pierside for more than 200 years.

Across from the market, under the elevated FDR Drive, is the Pier 17 Pavilion. Inside you will find more than 100 shops and restaurants. The view from the promenade is spectacular; upriver lie the Brooklyn and Manhattan bridges; across the East River is Brooklyn Heights (your ultimate destination); while downriver is the New York Harbor. You also have a great view of the historic ships moored at Piers 15 and 16. The tall ships are perhaps the most recognizable feature of the seaport. The grandest vessel there is the *Peking* (built in 1911), the second largest sailing ship in existence. All are worth a visit.

Return to the Fulton Street mall and continue down to Water Street. One block north, at Front and Beekman streets, you will find the Seaport's visitors' center, open daily except on Thanksgiving, Christmas, and New Year's Day. There you can learn of the many other attractions that await visitors to this fascinating part of New York City.

But now it is time for us to cast off. Pedal westward on Fulton to the intersection with Broadway, then make a right. (Note that since your route flows against the traffic on Broadway, you must dismount your bike and walk for one block.)

Across Broadway is **St. Paul's Chapel**, the oldest church in Manhattan. You can't miss it; the churchyard takes up the entire block. Most of the chapel was completed in 1766, though the spire and portico facing Broadway were constructed in 1794.

Take the next right onto Park Row and get back on your bike. Skirting the edge of City Hall Park, wind along Park Row as it heads toward the **Brooklyn Bridge**. Joining Centre Street, follow the signs as they lead toward the bridge's central bicycle/pedestrian path. Though the path begins with a climb, the outstanding view of lower Manhattan makes it worth the effort!

The Brooklyn Bridge was the first of the city's great bridges. In 1869 John Roebling was commissioned to design the bridge which had been branded "impossible." Though Roebling died before the bridge was finished, his son, Washington, directed the effort to its successful completion. When it opened in 1883, the Brooklyn Bridge was hailed as the "eighth wonder of the world," and it remains today as a monument to American creativity and genius.

Follow the bike-path signs as you descend the Brooklyn side of the bridge and take a right onto Tillary Street. Stay on the "diamond" bike lane as it winds westward. Turn right onto Cadman Plaza West, then left onto Clark Street to enter **Brooklyn Heights.** Home to the twin cousins Patty and Cathy Lane of the TV sitcom "The Patty Duke Show," Brooklyn Heights has retained much of its charm from a century ago, when it was Manhattan's first suburb.

After two short blocks turn left onto Henry Street. A narrow lane shaded by trees and lined with shoulder-to-shoulder homes, Henry typifies the streets of Brooklyn Heights. Continue to the intersection with Remsen Street, then sidestep for a quick visit to Our Lady of Lebanon Church. Adding to the uniqueness of its Romanesque Revival–style architecture are the church doors, salvaged from the shipwrecked ocean liner *Normandie.*

Back on Henry, watch for Hunts Lane, a small dead-end street on the left. Hunts Lane is a marvelous mews lined with a number of restored carriage houses that were once stables for the affluent residents of nearby Remsen Street.

Turn right twice, once onto Joralemon Street, then again, in one block, onto Hicks Street. There, you will pass Grace Church on the left and Grace Court Alley across the way. Like Hunts Lane, Grace Court Alley originally contained stables and carriage houses owned by wealthy local residents.

At Montague Street turn left and continue all the way to its end. You now have a choice to make. If you wish you may continue straight onto the Brooklyn Heights Promenade, but please bear in mind that bicycle riding is prohibited for its entire length. You wouldn't want to rush here, anyway. Take the time to enjoy the breathtaking view of the Manhattan skyline and lower New York Harbor. Trees, flowers, and benches line the promenade, making it a wonderful place for a midride break.

If you prefer to stay on your bike instead, turn right onto Pierrepont Place. At its end swerve left to continue on Columbia Heights. These two streets feature some of the finest brownstone homes in all of New York City.

Wind to the right onto Cranberry Street, then right again onto Willow Street. Some widely varied architecture adds to the delight of these residential roads. Especially noteworthy is the row of homes from 151 to 159 Willow Street. Though you would never guess it, a tunnel used to connect 159 and 151, the latter once being a stable.

A pair of quick lefts will take you from Willow to Pierrepont Street and finally onto Hicks Street, heading north again. You'll almost feel as if you're traveling through a fruit salad, as you pass streets with names like Pineapple and Orange. Just down Orange on the right is the Plymouth Church of the Pilgrims. The church played a key role in the Underground Railroad, which was used to smuggle slaves to freedom before the Civil War.

Stay on Hicks for 1 more block to Cranberry Street, where the route makes another right. A second right puts you back on Henry Street. Continue on Henry for 5 blocks, then turn left onto Pierrepont Street. Before leaving Brooklyn Heights stop at the **Brooklyn Historical Society's** home at the corner of Pierrepont and Clinton streets. Its collection of Brooklyn memorabilia ranges from playing equipment used by the Brooklyn Dodgers to a huge cast-iron eagle, once the symbol of the now-defunct *Brooklyn Eagle* newspaper. The society is open Tuesdays through Sundays and there is a nominal admission charge.

Turn left onto Cadman Plaza West, then right onto Tillary Street to join the Brooklyn Bridge bikeway. At the end of the bikeway, turn left onto Centre Street and proceed onto Park Row. Just before Broadway take a left onto Ann Street. A right in a couple of blocks onto Gold Street and a left onto Fulton Street will bring you back to the seaport. (If you wish, continue south on Broadway toward Battery Park and follow Ride #1 for an excursion into Greenwich Village.)

For Further Information

South Street Seaport (212) 669–9424
Brooklyn Historical Society (718) 624–0890

Getting There

The seaport is located at the intersection of Fulton and South streets, adjacent to the FDR Drive. If you must drive there, keep in mind that a parking spot can be difficult to come by. You might do better by parking along Tillary Street or another road near the Brooklyn side of the bridge.

Brooklyn
Brooklyn Greenway

Mileage:	22 or 35
Approximate pedaling time:	3 hours or 5 hours
Terrain:	Flat
Traffic:	Light in park and on bikeways, heavy elsewhere
Things to see:	Prospect Park, Grand Army Plaza, Brooklyn Botanic Garden, Brooklyn Public Library, Brooklyn Museum, Coney Island, New York Aquarium, Verrazano-Narrows Bridge

Even as you read this, ambitious plans are underfoot to create a "greenway" of hiking and biking trails that will extend for 40 miles, from the Atlantic Ocean at Coney Island in Brooklyn to the beginning of Long Island Sound at Fort Totten in Queens. Along the way the route will connect thirteen parks, two botanic gardens, three lakes, and many other cultural, historic, and recreational centers. This is the dream of the Neighborhood Open Space Coalition, a nonprofit group whose aim is to preserve and improve the city's outdoors. On this ride you will get a chance to preview some of the areas that will form the Brooklyn portion of the Greenway, while Ride #5 presents much of the Queens end of the Greenway.

Actually, this is two rides in one. Both originate from Park Circle, adjacent to the south entrance of **Prospect Park**. The first stage is a quick loop of the park itself. Proceed through the entrance and join the marked bike route as it travels counterclockwise along Park Drive.

The first thing you are bound to notice inside the park is Prospect

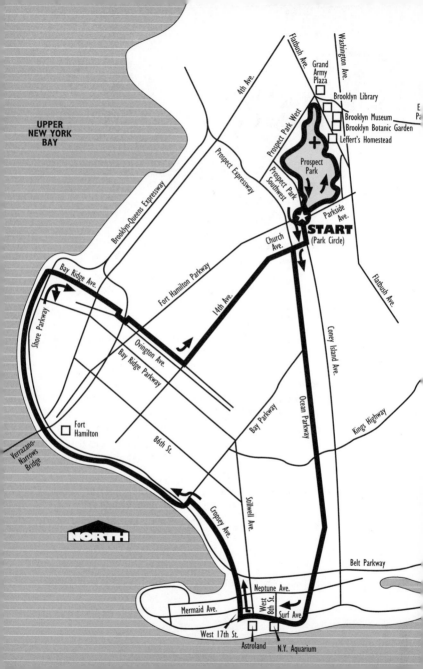

**DIREC-
TIONS
at a glance**

0.0	Begin at Park Circle. Enter park.
1.8	Top of park at Grand Army Plaza.
3.7	Exit park toward Park Circle. Travel counterclockwise around circle.
3.8	Right onto Coney Island Avenue.
4.1	Right onto Church Avenue.
4.3	Left onto Ocean Parkway bikeway.
9.1	Follow road to right onto Surf Avenue.
10.1	Right onto West 17th Street.
10.3	Cross Neptune Avenue and join Cropsey Avenue.
11.8	Left onto Bay Parkway.
12.0	Cross under Shore (Belt) Parkway and join bikeway on right.
16.7	Bikeway ends at pier opposite Bay Ridge Avenue. To return, either turn around or continue on Bay Ridge Avenue.
17.8	Right onto BQE service road.
17.9	Left onto Ovington Avenue.
18.0	Left onto 7th Avenue.
18.1	Right onto Bay Ridge Avenue.
18.9	Left onto 14th Avenue.
20.7	Veer right to continue on Church Avenue.
21.3	Left onto Coney Island Avenue.
21.6	Back at Park Circle.

Lake, a tranquil body of water surrounded by open meadow. The lake's boathouse, where visitors once rented boats for quiet afternoon cruises, acts as the park's visitors' center.

A little farther along Park Drive, off to the right, is Leffert's Homestead, a restored Dutch colonial farmhouse built in 1783. A museum inside features colonial furniture along with a variety of changing exhibits. The homestead is open weekends year-round as well as Wednesday through Friday from April through December.

A little ways past the right-hand turn toward Leffert's Homestead, get ready to pedal up the park's biggest climb. The hill tops out just before the park's north gate. Outside the gate, at the intersection of Flatbush Avenue and Eastern Parkway, is **Grand Army Plaza**. At the head of the plaza stands the majestic Triumphal Arch, which commemorates the Union's victory in the Civil War. Atop the arch is the sculpture of a mighty horse-drawn chariot, while statues of the army and navy adorn either side.

Across Flatbush Avenue from the plaza is the **Brooklyn Botanic Garden**. The grounds feature thousands of different species of flowers, trees, and bushes set in half a dozen theme gardens. Of special interest is the Steinhardt Conservatory, a magnificent complex of greenhouses simulating many contrasting environments. Admission to the garden is free, though there is a small charge to visit the conservatory.

Set at the southeastern corner of Eastern Parkway and Flatbush Avenue is the **Brooklyn Public Library**. Inside, more than 1.5 million volumes await bibliophiles. Next door to the library the **Brooklyn Museum** features an amazingly wide selection of exhibits throughout its five floors. These range from totem poles and masks to a granite sarcophagus dating to 2500 B.C. Be sure to stop at both of these fascinating places, but allow enough time for your visit.

Return to Prospect Park, continuing counterclockwise along the marked bike lane. Happily, this part of the path is downhill! Stay on the lane toward the south gate, where you will see signs leading toward Ocean Parkway and the ride's second stage to Coney Island— and, ultimately, into Bay Ridge.

Ocean Parkway was the world's second parkway when it opened in 1874. On June 15, 1895, the first-ever bikeway was opened to the cycling public. It ran along Ocean Parkway for 5 miles, from Prospect Park to Coney Island. On that inaugural day the League of American Wheelmen sponsored a ride that attracted more than 10,000 participants!

Due to construction along both Prospect Expressway and Ocean Parkway in 1974, the bikeway north of Church Avenue was almost completely eliminated. Getting from the park to the parkway is now a bit more complicated and a bit more hazardous. Here's how to do it: *Carefully* circle three-quarters of the way around Park Circle to Coney

Island Avenue; then turn right. Stay on Coney Island Avenue until you come to Church Avenue; take another right.

Once at the intersection of Church Avenue and Ocean Parkway, proceed southward on the bikeway, adjacent to the latter's southbound traffic lane. Trees overhang the route, offering cooling shade on what can be a hot route. A black metal divider runs the entire length of the bikeway in an attempt to keep pedestrians out of the cyclists' way and vice versa. Please observe the rule that restricts bike riding to one-half of the path only (the half closer to the parkway).

Bear right at the end of the bikeway onto Surf Avenue. Welcome to **Coney Island!** The name immediately conjures up images of thundering roller coasters, giant Ferris wheels, and hot dogs galore, but when the Dutch first landed here in the early 1600s, all they found were rabbits. The island was full of them. In fact, the name *Coney Island* is an Americanized version of the original Dutch name, *Konijn Eiland,* meaning "rabbit island."

By the 1830s the rabbits had been replaced by elegant hotels, lavish casinos, and throngs of wealthy beach goers. The 1880s saw Coney Island change dramatically as the resort turned into a huge amusement park.

Though the area fell on hard times beginning in the 1950s, a few of the original rides remain open. And you can still get a hot dog from the first "Nathan's Famous" hot dog stand, though it will cost more than the nickel Nathan Handwerker used to charge.

The **New York Aquarium** relocated to Coney Island from Manhattan's Battery Park in 1957. Located on the corner of Surf Avenue and West 8th Street, the aquarium features both indoor and outdoor exhibits. Inside, you can see more than 300 species of fishes, while outside, large tanks hold whales, dolphins, sea lions, and penguins. The aquarium is open daily, with a modest admission charge.

Though the Greenway ends here, our route continues. Across from the rusting remains of the Coney Island Parachute Jump, turn right onto West 17th Street and cross Coney Island Inlet to join Cropsey Avenue. Stay on Cropsey for 1.5 miles to the intersection with Bay Parkway. Turn left and go under Shore Parkway (a.k.a. Belt Parkway). When you emerge on the other side, you will find yourself in a huge parking lot. Ahead are two large buildings; one houses Caesar's Bay Bazaar, the other, a Toys-R-Us store. As you enter the lot look to the right for a small sign leading to Shore Bikeway.

The bikeway closely follows the curved shoreline of Brooklyn. Across the water you can see South Beach on Staten Island, while looming up ahead is the **Verrazano-Narrows Bridge**. Opened in November 1964, the Verrazano spans 13,700 feet, the longest span of any suspension bridge.

Dwarfed by the Verrazano is Fort Wadsworth, which teamed with Fort Hamilton in Brooklyn to defend the port of New York against invasion during colonial times.

The bikeway ends at a concrete pier that juts out into the harbor. From here you have a dramatic view of lower Manhattan, Staten Island, the Statue of Liberty, Ellis Island, and the Verrazano.

To return to Prospect Park you may either reverse the route or cut across Brooklyn on any of a number of different roads (the map offers one possibility). If you choose the latter, please keep in mind that much of the road surface in this area is rutted and potentially damaging to delicate touring bicycles. Mountain bikers, on the other hand, may find the terrain invigorating, but be especially watchful of traffic.

For Further Information

Prospect Park (718) 788–0055
Brooklyn Botanic Garden (718) 622–4433
Brooklyn Public Library (718) 780–7700
New York Aquarium (718) 266–8711

Getting There

Park Circle lies near the intersection of Fort Hamilton Parkway, Ocean Parkway, and Prospect Expressway. The latter is directly accessible from the Brooklyn–Queens Expressway (Interstate 278). Parking is most readily available along Parkside Avenue (Prospect Park's south border).

5 Queens
Queens Greenway

Mileage:	24 (round trip)
Approximate pedaling time:	4 hours
Terrain:	Rolling
Traffic:	Light to moderate (nonexistent on bikeways)
Things to see:	Queens Museum, Flushing Meadows–Corona Park, Unisphere, New York Hall of Science, Queens Botanical Garden, Kissena Park, Cunningham Park, Alley Pond Park, Alley Pond Environmental Center

As mentioned at the beginning of Ride #4, the Brooklyn-Queens Greenway is the ambitious plan of the Neighborhood Open Space Coalition to link thirteen city parks with a series of hiking and biking trails. On this ride you will travel either on or parallel to the Greenway as it stretches from Flushing Meadows–Corona Park to Fort Totten and Clearview Park in Bayside.

Begin from the parking lot of the **Queens Museum** in **Flushing Meadows–Corona Park.** The Queens Museum, located in the New York City Building, is open daily except Mondays. It features a highly detailed scale model of the city as well as many changing art exhibits.

Centrally located within Flushing Meadows–Corona Park is the **Unisphere**, symbol of the outstanding world's fair held here in 1964–65. Flushing Meadows was also the site of the equally notable 1939–40 world's fair. In fact, it was this first spectacular that led city parks commissioner Robert Moses to transform the area magically from an ash dump to a beautiful park setting.

The **New York Hall of Science** is located in the park at 111th

29

DIREC-TIONS at a glance

0.0 Begin at Unisphere, heading east on park path.
0.3 Cross under Clearview Expressway, over College Point Boulevard, and into Kissena Park Corridor.
0.8 Exit Kissena Park Corridor; turn left onto Main Street.
0.9 Right onto Elder Avenue.
1.0 Right onto Colden Street.
1.5 Left onto Oak Avenue.
1.9 Right onto Bowne Street.
2.0 Straight across Rose Avenue and into Kissena Park.
2.4 Exit park, crossing 164th Street and continuing on Underhill Avenue.
2.7 Left onto 170th Street.
2.8 Right onto Lithonia Avenue (shortly changes names back to Underhill).
3.6 Cross 58th Avenue and switch to park path.
3.8 Cross bridge over Long Island Expressway.
3.9 Follow path toward right, walking to Peck Avenue.
4.0 Left onto Peck Avenue (becomes 199th Street).
4.4 Left onto 73rd Avenue.
4.7 Right onto Hollis Hills Terrace.
5.0 Left onto old Vanderbilt Motor Parkway.
6.6 Follow arrows from Motor Parkway through Alley Pond Park; then turn left onto Winchester Boulevard (changes name to Douglaston Parkway at top of hill).
7.7 Left onto West Alley Road.
7.9 Right onto Easthampton Boulevard.
8.6 Left onto Horatio Parkway.
8.9 Right onto Cloverdale Avenue.
9.1 Right onto 223rd Street.
9.2 Right onto Northern Boulevard (Route 25A).
9.5 After crossing Cross Island Parkway, left onto path leading to "Joe Michael's Mile" bikeway.
12.0 Bikeway ends at Fort Totten.

Street and 48th Avenue, on the other side of Grand Central Parkway. To get there take the foot bridge just south of the museum parking lot. The hall features a wide array of "user-friendly" exhibits that invite visitors to participate in the action. Displays cover a broad range of topics in all of the sciences. The hall is open Wednesdays through Sundays; there is a small admission fee.

Back across Grand Central Parkway head south on the park paths toward Meadow Lake and Willow Lake. Then circle back north along the park's eastern boundary toward Shea Stadium and the U.S. Tennis Association's stadium, home of the U.S. Open Tennis Championships. Next door to the pitch-and-putt golf course is a bicycle rental stand, which will come in handy if you are bikeless and wish to join in with the other pedalers. Call (718) 699–9598 for information.

Miles and miles of paved trails are found within Flushing Meadows–Corona Park. They, along with the attractions described above, make it easy to spend hours on a bicycle without ever leaving the park. But we must push on, for there is much to see outside of the park as well.

From the Unisphere head east along the park's paths toward the elevated Van Wyck Expressway (Interstate 678). Follow the trail under the expressway and into Kissena Park Corridor, a long, thin stretch of parkland wedged between the bustling roads of Flushing. Almost immediately after emerging from under the Van Wyck Expressway, you face one of the greatest uphill challenges of the ride as the path crosses over College Point Boulevard. The bridge is short but steep and difficult to scale if you are not prepared. The trip down the other side is invigorating, but beware of bumps where the bridge meets the ground.

Continue along the bike path through Kissena Park Corridor, avoiding any sharp turns to the left or right (these lead to local roads). About 0.5 mile later you will come to the entrance of the **Queens Botanical Garden.** Constructed in 1964, the facility features thirty-eight acres of colorful gardens and educational floral exhibits.

Past the Botanical Garden the bikeway comes to an abrupt end on Main Street. Joining traffic, continue to wind your way from Main onto Elder Avenue, Colden Street, and Oak Avenue.

Enter **Kissena Park** across from the intersection of Bowne Street and Rose Avenue. For the purpose of measuring the ride's mileage, we stayed along the northern path around Kissena Park, but you may want to tour the other bike paths as well.

Leave Kissena Park through one of its eastern exits, cross 164th Street, and continue on Underhill Avenue. After crossing 58th Avenue shift from Underhill to the paved path in Peck Corridor Park on the right. As Underhill ends at the westbound Horace Harding Expressway (the service road adjacent to the Long Island Expressway), follow the path up and over both it and the Long Island Expressway (Interstate 495).

The path ends on the other side of the bridge, forcing riders onto the heavily traveled eastbound Horace Harding Expressway. Dismount and walk your bike, following the path to the right (against traffic). Take the first left onto Peck Avenue, which later changes names to 199th Street. This stretch of 199th Street slices along the edge of **Cunningham Park.**

At the next intersection, turn left onto 73rd Avenue. Cross Francis Lewis Boulevard at the next intersection and continue through the park. Veer right immediately after passing under the Clearview Expressway (Interstate 295) onto Hollis Hills Terrace. Not far ahead, just before passing under a white bridge, turn left onto an unmarked paved path that heads into the woods. This is the western entrance to the old Vanderbilt Motor Parkway, which was constructed in 1906. Today few portions of its 48 original miles still exist. Fortunately, this section, which connects Cunningham Park to Alley Pond Park, has been preserved by the city as a traffic-free path to be enjoyed by cyclists, joggers, and pedestrians.

As the preserved parkway draws to a close, follow the painted arrows on the road into **Alley Pond Park.** The second largest park in Queens, Alley Pond Park boasts 623 acres of woods and meadows. At the end of the park road, turn left onto Winchester Boulevard and pass under Grand Central Parkway. The road now changes names to Douglaston Parkway and winds its way uphill, cresting in about 0.5 mile.

Although there are no paved bicycle trails to follow, the route tracks Alley Pond Park all the way to Northern Boulevard (Route 25A). On the way you will pass Oakland Lake on the right.

Crossing over the Cross Island Parkway, continue on Northern

Boulevard until you come to the **Alley Pond Environmental Center**. The center, open daily, features both indoor and outdoor exhibits.

From the nature center turn left and backtrack on Northern Boulevard for 0.25 mile. As you approach the Cross Island Parkway, turn right onto the "Joe Michael's Mile" bikeway. The bikeway parallels the northbound Cross Island Parkway and offers striking views of Little Neck Bay, Port Washington, and the distant Bronx. Along the way you will pass the Bayside Yacht Club.

The bikeway empties onto Totten Road, adjacent to the Fort Totten Army base. Fort Totten was completed in 1857, not long before the Civil War, ironically enough from a design by Robert E. Lee. Pause to catch both your breath and the spectacular view of the Throgs Neck Bridge. Then it's back on the bike for the reverse trip home to Flushing Meadows–Corona Park.

For Further Information

Flushing Meadows–Corona Park (718) 507–3117
Queens Museum (718) 592–2405
New York Hall of Science (718) 699–0005
Kissena Park Nature Center (718) 353–1047
Queens Botanical Garden (718) 886–3800
Alley Pond Environmental Center (718) 229–4000

Getting There

To reach the ride's starting point, take the Flushing Meadows–Corona Park/Shea Stadium exit off Grand Central Parkway, bearing right at the end of the exit ramp into the park. Do not attempt this when a ball game is scheduled—you'll never make it! The Long Island Railroad's Port Washington line services Flushing with frequent stops. From the Shea Stadium station enter the park and proceed to the Queens Museum.

Bronx
Van Cortlandt Park to Pelham Bay Park

Mileage:	7 (one way)
Approximate pedaling time:	1 hour, without side trips through parks
Terrain:	Mostly flat
Traffic:	Potentially heavy along portions of Mosholu and Pelham parkways, moderate elsewhere
Things to see:	Van Cortlandt Park, New York Botanical Garden, Fordham University, Bronx Zoo, Pelham Bay Park

Named for Jonas Bronk, who first settled in 1639 between today's Harlem and Bronx rivers, the Bronx presents some unusual challenges to city cyclists. In this borough of social contrasts, you will find ghetto and grandeur only a few miles apart. Some of the roads are pitted with holes that a cyclist could almost get lost in, while others are silky smooth. The Bronx is, indeed, a borough of sharp divergence.

Begin your ride in **Van Cortlandt Park,** a park rich in both natural and historical significance. Within its 1,146 acres you will find miles of roads and paths on which to cycle. One of the many sights you will find within the park is the Van Cortlandt Mansion, the oldest building in the Bronx. The mansion appears much as it did in 1748, the year it was built. Inside, each room is outfitted with authentic period furniture. Perhaps you can even imagine George Washington standing inside. He used the mansion as a meeting place during the American Revolution.

Of the many nature trails scattered throughout the park, two of the most interesting are the Aqueduct and the Old Putnam Railroad trails. The Aqueduct trail follows an aqueduct built in the 1830s to bring water to the city from the Croton reservoirs in Westchester

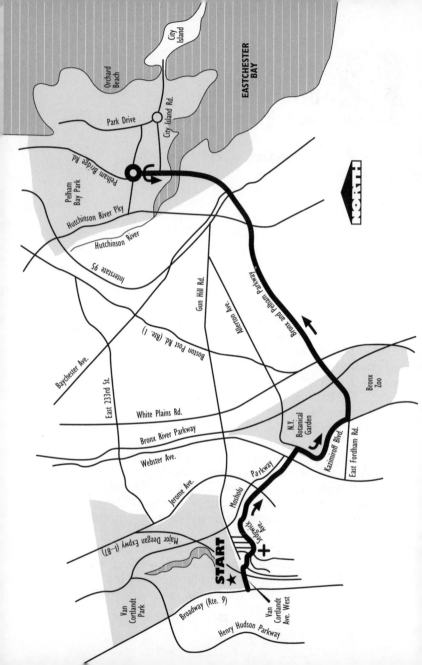

DIREC-TIONS at a glance

0.0	Left onto Van Cortlandt Park South from the south exit of Van Cortlandt Park.
0.3	Right onto Van Cortlandt Avenue West.
0.5	Left onto Sedgewick Avenue.
0.8	Right onto Mosholu Parkway.
1.9	Right onto Dr. Theodore Kazimiroff Boulevard.
2.8	Left onto East Fordham Road (U.S. Route 1).
3.2	Join Bronx and Pelham Parkway (see text).
6.4	Cross Hutchinson River into Pelham Bay Park.
7.1	Ride ends at traffic circle, but riders are encouraged to explore the park's many paved roads.

County. The trail continues beyond the park's northern perimeter all the way to the Croton Dam.

The Old Putnam Railroad trail cuts the park in half. Since the last trains roared across its tracks in the late 1950s, the railroad bed has been transformed into a pleasant trail for hikers and mountain bikers.

Proceed out of the park's south exit and get ready to scale the heights of Van Cortlandt Avenue West as it heads toward Sedgewick Avenue and Mosholu Parkway. The latter, a wide, multilane road, takes you south toward Dr. Theodore Kazimiroff Boulevard and the New York Botanical Garden.

The **New York Botanical Garden** is world famous for its lush environs. Inside its rolling terrain is the Hemlock Forest, the Bronx River Gorge and Falls, and forty acres of virgin woodland. You can tiptoe through the tulips (well, not actually through, but near) daily for free. Lock your bike to the rack found near the entrance and enjoy the extraordinary grounds and buildings.

Follow Kazimiroff Boulevard counterclockwise around the garden, passing the **Fordham University** campus on the right. At the next intersection turn left onto East Fordham Road (U. S. Route 1 north). On the corner is the entrance to the New York Zoological Park, better known as the **Bronx Zoo**. The zoo hosts more than 4,000 animals in both indoor and outdoor habitats that simulate everything from darkest Africa to the Arctic. Open daily from 10 A.M. until around 5 P.M.,

37

PELHAM BAY PARK

City of New York   Parks & Recreation

the park may be toured by foot, safari train, or monorail. A nominal admission fee is charged, and there is an additional fee for certain attractions. It sure is easy to spend an entire day at the zoo!

Continue east on East Fordham Road (watch out for heavy traffic) and the Bronx and Pelham Bikeway. The bikeway heads east adjacent to the north side of the Bronx and Pelham Parkway. The center divider ends in 2 miles; at this point, cross back to the south side of the road to continue on the paved path.

Carefully traverse the metal-grated bridge over the Hutchinson River into **Pelham Bay Park.** Miles of trails are waiting to bring the enthusiastic cyclist around the park. For hikers there is the Thomas Pell Wildlife Refuge, a wonderful environmental center named for the area's first permanent resident from Europe. For historians there is the Bartow-Pell Mansion, completed in 1842 by Robert Bartow, a descendant of Pell. And you must take a side trip to Orchard Beach, which has been described as the "Riviera of New York."

Make a final loop around the park and cross back over Pelham Bridge. Then it's back along Pelham Parkway to Van Cortlandt Park.

For Further Information

Van Cortlandt Park (212) 543–3344
New York Botanical Garden (212) 220–8700
Bronx Zoo (212) 220–5100
Pelham Bay Park (212) 430–1890

Getting There

Van Cortlandt Park can be reached from exits off Mosholu Parkway, the Major Deegan Expressway (Van Cortlandt Park South exit to Route 9), or the Henry Hudson Parkway (Exit 23). Regardless of the highway used, follow the signs to the park's entrance. You will find parking along neighboring streets and in the park at the golf course.

Staten Island
Grymes Hill to Snug Harbor

Mileage:	8
Approximate pedaling time:	1.5 hours
Terrain:	Hilly
Traffic:	Moderate
Things to see:	Wagner College, Clove Lakes Park, Staten Island Zoo, Snug Harbor Cultural Center, Silver Lake Park

Although it has grown considerably since the opening of the Verrazano-Narrows Bridge in 1964, Staten Island remains the most rural of the city's five boroughs. Its pleasant blend of big-city and suburban charms allows city cyclists to enjoy the best of both worlds right in their own backyards.

Begin along Howard Avenue atop Grymes Hill, the second highest hill on Staten Island. Commanding center stage amid the beautiful homes and numerous garden apartments on Grymes Hill is **Wagner College**. The Wagner campus is noted for its countrylike beauty and, in sharp contrast, its commanding view of lower Manhattan, the Verrazano-Narrows Bridge, Brooklyn, and the New York Harbor. We are both especially fond of Wagner College. It was here, as undergraduate students, that we first met on a snowy night in January 1978 (no, we were *not* riding bicycles at the time).

Coast down Grymes Hill on Howard Avenue. Don't build up too much speed on the way down, since you must stop at the bottom and turn right onto Clove Road. You will soon arrive at the four-way intersection at Clove and Victory Boulevard. Turn left onto Victory; then, just ahead on the right, steer into **Clove Lakes Park**. Actually, there are several paved paths into the park from which you may choose. You might prefer to ride along the shore of Clove Lake itself or to cycle

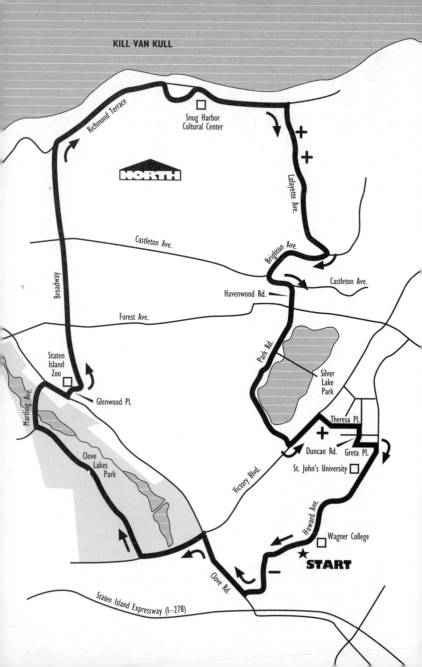

DIREC-TIONS at a glance

0.0	Begin on Howard Avenue across from Wagner College.
0.3	Right onto Clove Road.
0.7	Left onto Victory Boulevard.
1.0	Right into Clove Lakes Park.
1.4	Right onto Martling Avenue.
1.6	Right onto Clove Road.
1.7	Left onto Glenwood Place.
1.8	Left onto Broadway.
2.9	Right onto Richmond Terrace.
3.3	Stay to the left on Richmond Terrace.
4.2	Right onto Lafayette Avenue.
4.9	Right onto Brighton Avenue.
5.2	Left onto Castleton Avenue.
5.3	Right onto Havenwood Street.
5.4	Straight into Silver Lake Park Road.
6.2	Left onto Victory Boulevard.
6.3	Right onto Theresa Place.
6.6	Right onto Duncan Road.
6.8	Left onto Greta Place.
6.9	Right onto Howard Avenue.
7.5	Back at Wagner College.

through the park's adjacent woodlands. And if you just happen to have a pair of ice skates with you, there is always the park's ice rink.

Exiting from Clove Lakes Park, turn right onto Martling Avenue and right again onto Clove Road. Watch for the **Staten Island Zoo** across from the intersection between Martling and Clove Road. The zoo has something for everyone. Outside is a pony track and barn and exhibits featuring flamingos, otters, raccoons, and porcupines. Indoor displays include a marvelous aquarium, a serpentarium, and a soon-to-be-opened tropical rain forest. For kids a petting zoo lets everyone feed goats and watch ducks dive into their pond. The zoo is open daily from 10 A.M. to 4:45 P.M., with entrances on both Clove Road and Broadway. A small admission fee is charged.

The route turns left onto Glenwood Place, then left again onto Broadway. Broadway will lead you all the way to Richmond Terrace and the Kill Van Kull, a narrow strip of water that marks the north shore of Staten Island. Turn right on Richmond Terrace and continue for 0.7 mile, where you will meet Snug Harbor Road and the **Snug Harbor Cultural Center** on the right. Founded in 1801, Snug Harbor was the nation's first maritime hospital and home for retired sailors. Today, its twenty-eight buildings and eighty acres comprise a wonderful park setting.

Back on Richmond Terrace the route winds inland along Lafayette, Brighton, and Castleton avenues. Bordering Forest Avenue to the south is **Silver Lake Park,** another pleasant city park for cycling. Follow Silver Lake Park Road past the lake itself. For a beautiful view shoot off onto the path that crosses the dam in the middle of Silver Lake.

Emerging from the other side of the park, turn left onto Victory Boulevard, then right on Theresa Place for the final climb up Grymes Hill. Back on Howard Avenue you will pass many regal homes as well as the Staten Island campus of Saint John's University. Once past Saint John's, continue on Howard back to the Wagner College campus.

For Further Information

Wagner College (718) 390–3100
Clove Lakes Park (718) 390–8031
Staten Island Zoo (718) 442–3101
Snug Harbor Cultural Center (718) 448–2500
Silver Lake Park (718) 816–5466

Getting There

Howard Avenue can be reached by taking the Clove Road exit off the Staten Island Expressway (Interstate 278). Those coming from Manhattan can take the Staten Island Ferry to the Saint George terminal, then follow Victory Boulevard to Theresa Place.

Staten Island
Great Kills to South Beach and Todt Hill

Mileage:	20
Approximate pedaling time:	3 hours
Terrain:	Flat, except for Todt Hill
Traffic:	Moderate
Things to see:	Great Kills Park, Richmondtown Restoration, Midland Beach, South Beach, Todt Hill, High Rock Conservation Center

The eastern shore of Staten Island has something for every bicyclist. For the seasoned pedaler there are challenging uphill climbs, while for the leisure rider there are long, flat expanses with little or no traffic. On this ride you will experience both.

The tour opens with a visit to **Great Kills Park**, part of the Gateway National Recreation Area. Gateway is made up of four park units along the coast adjacent to New York Harbor. Great Kills Park is formed from a peninsula jutting out into Lower New York Bay. Once the site of an Algonquin Indian village, the land was purchased in 1860 by one John Crooke. Crooke, a reclusive mining engineer and naturalist, made his home at the peninsula's tip, now known as Crooke's Point. New York City purchased the land in 1929 and opened Great Kills Park twenty years later. In 1974 park jurisdiction was transferred to the National Park Service, which has maintained it ever since.

The park's natural habitat is home to many coastal plants and animals. Along some of the footpaths you will find seaside goldenrod, bayberry, prickly pear, and several other unique flora. Hiding among the dunes and gullies are squirrels, rabbits, turtles, ring-necked pheas-

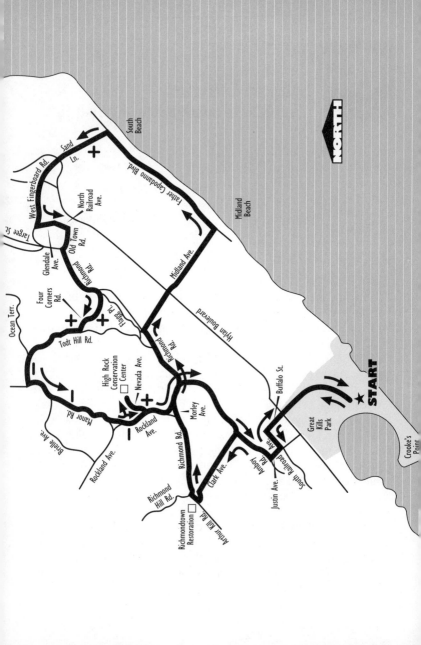

DIREC-TIONS at a glance

0.0	Begin at Great Kills Park visitors' center.
1.0	Cross Hylan Boulevard onto Buffalo Street.
1.3	Left onto South Railroad Avenue.
1.5	Right onto Justin Avenue.
1.7	Right onto Amboy Road.
2.2	Left onto Clarke Avenue.
3.1	Right onto Arthur Kill Road.
3.3	Right onto Richmond Road.
4.3	Straight onto Morley Avenue.
4.5	Straight onto Richmond Road.
4.7	Left to stay on Richmond Road.
5.5	Right onto Midland Avenue.
6.8	Left onto Father Capodanno Boulevard.
8.6	Left onto Sand Lane.
9.3	Straight onto West Fingerboard Road.
10.2	Left onto Glendale Avenue.
10.4	Straight onto North Railroad Avenue.
10.6	Right onto Old Town Road.
10.9	Left onto Richmond Road.
11.4	Right onto Four Corners Road. Continue to the right at the stop sign just ahead to stay on Four Corners Road.
12.1	Right onto Todt Hill Road.
12.8	Left onto Ocean Terrace.
13.1	Left onto Manor Road.
14.2	Left onto Rockland Avenue.
14.8	Left onto Nevada Avenue to end; turn around.
16.2	Left back onto Rockland Avenue.
16.4	Left onto Richmond Road.
16.8	Right onto Amboy Road.
18.3	Left onto Justin Avenue.
18.4	Left onto South Railroad Avenue.
18.6	Right onto Buffalo Street.
18.9	Straight into Great Kills Park.
19.9	Return to visitors' center.

ants, and many other small animals. If you choose to venture along one of the trails, please observe the park rule that bicycles are strictly prohibited.

Leave the park along its lone entrance road. Cross Hylan Boulevard and join Buffalo Street. Follow Buffalo until it ends at the Staten Island Rapid Transit tracks; then take a left on South Railroad Avenue. In three blocks turn right on Justin Avenue. Follow Justin as it passes under the orange railroad bridge and all the way to Amboy Road; turn right. Homes line the eastern side of Amboy Road, while a large cemetery takes up a good part of the other side.

About 0.25 mile after the cemetery ends, take a left onto Clarke Avenue. Though it begins on a commercial note, Clarke quickly changes into a residential road with a suburban flavor.

Just before Clarke ends at Arthur Kill Road, turn right into **Richmondtown Restoration**. Richmondtown re-creates the Staten Island of colonial days. Throughout its 100 acres the restoration features fourteen buildings outfitted with period furnishings and informative exhibits. Guides perform tasks that were once part of everyday life on the island. Be sure to stop at the Staten Island Historical Society's museum and store, located at 441 Clarke Avenue. The store offers a wide range of unique gifts and souvenirs, from pewter jewelry to teddy bears. The restoration is open Wednesday through Sunday as well as Monday holidays, and there is an admission charge. Allow between one and two hours for a complete tour.

Leave Richmondtown on Richmond Road heading east. Two confusing intersections lie ahead. As Richmond Road temporarily veers to the left, continue straight on Morley Avenue for 0.2 mile, then rejoin Richmond. The second uncertain junction occurs at the T intersection with Amboy Road. As Amboy peels off to the right, follow the green-and-white BIKE ROUTE sign toward the left to stay on Richmond.

Entering the Grant City part of the island, turn right onto one-way Midland Avenue. After crossing Hylan Boulevard Midland becomes a two-way road featuring a separate bike lane on the right. Be watchful of any cars parked between the bike lane and the curb. Follow Midland until it ends at Father Capodanno Boulevard. Turn left and join the adjacent bikeway. Paralleling the road on the right are

Midland Beach and **South Beach.** From the boardwalk that connects the two beaches you will enjoy a great view of Brooklyn across the harbor, with Coney Island on the right, Fort Hamilton straight ahead, and the Verrazano-Narrows Bridge off to the left. Do not ride on the boardwalk, however, as splinters from the wood have been known to puncture tires!

Just before the end of the bikeway, turn left onto Sand Lane and begin the climb toward Hylan Boulevard. Cross Hylan to join West Fingerboard Road. After traversing the railroad tracks turn left onto Glendale Avenue. Continue onto North Railroad Avenue until it ends at Old Town Road. Take a right onto Old Town and proceed to its end at Richmond Road. Turning left onto Richmond, get ready to face one of the most challenging parts of this ride—challenging not because of any great hills but because it's a narrow, bumpy, heavily traveled road. Exercise extreme caution as you pedal along this stretch.

Turn right onto Four Corners Road and start the ascent up **Todt Hill**—and we do mean up! Todt Hill rises more than 400 feet above sea level, making it the second highest point on the east coast. (If you want to avoid the climb, continue on Richmond and pick up the route ahead at Amboy Road.) When Four Corners Road ends, take a right onto Todt Hill Road to continue the climb toward the peak.

Veer left onto Ocean Terrace, followed by another left onto Manor Road to begin the descent of Todt Hill. Up ahead the road forks, with Manor continuing to the right. You want to stay to the left to join Rockland Avenue. Don't build up too much speed, because you'll turn left again just ahead.

That left puts you on Nevada Avenue, heading up toward **High Rock Conservation Center.** That's right, to get to the nature center, you have to climb back up part of Todt Hill. Sorry about that! But the trip is worth it, because High Rock, which the U.S. Department of the Interior has designated a National Environmental Education Landmark, is a one-of-a-kind place on Staten Island. Throughout its seventy-two acres of rich forest you will find a number of hiking trails, interpretive exhibits, and a unique garden for the blind. The center is open daily from 9 A.M. to 5 P.M. There is no charge for admission.

Back on Rockland Avenue, continue to its end at Richmond Road.

Turn right onto Amboy Road. Stay on Amboy until you arrive back at Justin Avenue. A left onto Justin followed by another left onto South Railroad Avenue and a right onto Buffalo returns you to Hylan Boulevard and, across the way, Great Kills Park.

For Further Information

Great Kills Park (718) 351–8700
Richmondtown Restoration (718) 351–1617
High Rock Conservation Center (718) 667–6042

Getting There

To get to Great Kills Park, take the Hylan Boulevard exit off the Staten Island Expressway (Interstate 278) just before the Verrazano Bridge. Travel south on Hylan for about 5 miles to the park's entrance on the left.

Nassau County
Bethpage Bikeway and Beyond

Mileage:	23
Approximate pedaling time:	3 hours
Terrain:	Flat on bikeway, rolling elsewhere
Traffic:	Light (nonexistent on bikeway)
Things to see:	Massapequa Preserve, Bethpage State Park, Quaker Cemetery, Old Bethpage Village Restoration, Battle Row Park (camping optional)

June 30, 1899, was an important date in Long Island bicycling history. That was the day that Brooklyn's Charles Murphy accepted the challenge to pedal 1 mile in one minute. Murphy rode on a special wooden track laid between the rails of the Long Island Railroad stretching between Bethpage and Babylon. He chose to follow a specially outfitted train designed to act as a windbreak. In the end Murphy had cycled the mile in 57.8 seconds, setting a record that held for forty years.

While we may admire Murphy's great accomplishment, we are certainly not out to challenge it. Our ride into and through the area will be at a much more leisurely pace. The Long Island Railroad does, however, offer a convenient starting point. Park at the Massapequa railroad station, an ideal place to disembark. Just look for the BETH-PAGE BIKEWAY signs beyond the station's eastern end. The bikeway offers a pleasant, traffic-free ride between Massapequa and Bethpage State Park. (Just watch out for other cyclists, pedestrians, and the occasional dog.) First, why not stop at a local deli and pick up something for lunch, since the bikeway ends at the state park's picnic area.

The first half of Bethpage Bikeway meanders through **Massape-**

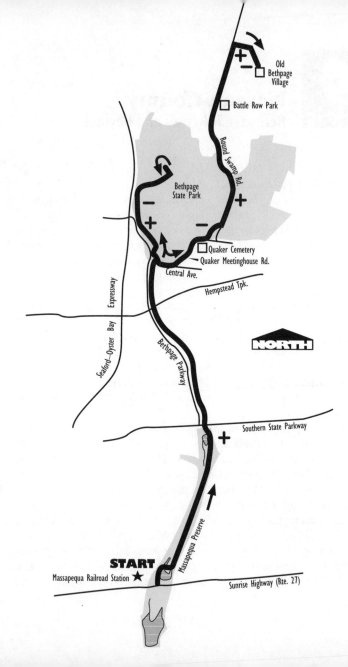

Old
Bethpage
Village

Battle Row Park

Round Swamp Rd.

Bethpage
State Park

Quaker Cemetery
Quaker Meetinghouse Rd.
Central Ave.

Hempstead Tpk.

NORTH

Seaford–Oyster Bay Expressway

Bethpage Parkway

Southern State Parkway

Massapequa Preserve

START
Massapequa Railroad Station ★

Sunrise Highway (Rte. 27)

DIREC-TIONS at a glance

0.0	Head north from the Massapequa railroad station on Bethpage Bikeway.
6.6	Bikeway ends at Bethpage State Park picnic area. Turn around.
8.3	Left onto exit ramp toward Central Avenue.
8.4	Left onto Central Avenue.
8.8	Left onto Quaker Meetinghouse Road.
9.5	Left onto Round Swamp Road.
12.2	Right into Old Bethpage Village Restoration. To return, turn left out the restoration exit.
14.9	Right onto Quaker Meetinghouse Road.
15.6	Right onto Central Avenue.
16.0	Right onto northbound entrance ramp to Bethpage Parkway.
16.1	Left onto southbound Bikeway (stay off the parkway!).
22.8	Welcome back to the Massapequa railroad station.

qua Preserve. This nature lover's oasis is wedged between Sunrise Highway and the Southern State Parkway. The bikeway rolls through the preserve along the west bank of a small pond, where children of all ages go fishing.

The path continues, following a stream to the north. Along the way small dams create ponds and marshes that abound with birds and waterfowl. During the spring and summer, wildflowers blossom throughout the preserve, adding color to the land and a delightful scent to the air.

As Massapequa Preserve ends the bikeway continues northward alongside Bethpage State Parkway. The only hill you will encounter before entering **Bethpage State Park** is the bridge up and over the Southern State Parkway; it is short but steep. Note that while the path remains separated from the road, it does cross each entrance and exit ramp. Riders *must* stop at each intersection and yield the right-of-way to automobile traffic. Be careful.

Once inside the park the bikeway continues all the way to the picnic area. This calls for lunch! Afterward, explore some of the park on foot. You will find ball fields and golf courses galore throughout its 1,475 acres.

Leave the park the same way you entered it. At the Central Avenue exit on the northbound side of Bethpage Parkway, turn left and carefully ride (or walk) to the ramp's end, where you will turn left. Keep turning to the left, winding from Central onto Quaker Meetinghouse Road. At the top of a rather long hill on Quaker Meetinghouse Road is another entrance into Bethpage Park. Inside are tennis courts and a clubhouse.

Across from the park entrance is the **Quaker Cemetery**. At the east end of the cemetery is the Quaker meetinghouse itself. While it is a new construction, a state historical marker indicates that meetings have been held at the site since 1698.

Bear left onto Round Swamp Road. Pedaling up a slow grade, slice through two of Bethpage Park's golf courses on your way northward.

In about 3 miles watch on the right for **Old Bethpage Village**. Follow the 0.5-mile-long entrance road into the restoration and secure your bike to one of the racks near the reception center. Inside are exhibits, a gift shop, and a cafeteria. Entering the village itself, you will feel as though you have passed through a time warp. Old Bethpage Village is an authentic re-creation of a nineteenth-century farming community, with the oldest building dating to 1765. All structures have been moved to the restoration from their original sites throughout Long Island.

Among the more interesting buildings in the village are the general store, the country inn, and the farm. Guides dressed in clothing of the period are eager to tell visitors about each of the village's forty-five buildings scattered over the 200-acre site. You should allow at least two hours to tour Old Bethpage Village, so plan your day accordingly.

For the more adventurous, **Battle Row Park** has camping facilities, which will enable you to turn this ride into an overnighter. Bicycle camping is a unique experience, one that every cyclist should try at least once. Be sure to telephone ahead for reservations.

The return trip follows Round Swamp Road back toward Bethpage State Park. To get back on the bikeway, carefully ride (or walk) down the northbound entrance ramp to Bethpage Parkway off Central Avenue. Just before the ramp merges onto the parkway, turn left at the BIKE ROUTE sign for the return trip to the Massapequa railroad station.

For Further Information

Bethpage State Park (516) 249–0701
Old Bethpage Village (516) 420–5280
Battle Row Park (516) 293–7120

Getting There

The ride begins at the Massapequa railroad station, located at the intersection of Sunrise Highway (Route 27) and Broadway. Metered parking (free on weekends and holidays) is available near the station. For those who prefer mass transit, the Long Island Railroad's main line makes frequent stops here.

Nassau County
Greenvale to Old Westbury

Mileage:	16
Approximate pedaling time:	3 hours
Terrain:	Hilly
Traffic:	Heavy in Roslyn, light to moderate elsewhere
Things to see:	Louis Clark Nature Refuge, New York Institute of Technology, C. W. Post College, Old Westbury Gardens and Mansion, Roslyn Park, Ward Clock Tower, Cedarmere

The north shore of Nassau County is frequently called the "Gold Coast" of Long Island and with good reason. The small villages, from Port Washington in the west to Oyster Bay in the east, all espouse large estates, elite shops (or is that *shoppes?*), and exotic cars. As you hobnob with the rich and famous by bicycle, just remember this one bit of advice (borrowed, with apologies, from the Old West): "There are hills in them thar gold!"

Begin the ride from the Greenvale railroad station on Greenvale–Glen Cove Avenue. Just ahead the road splits into a divided highway, but one with an ample shoulder for safe cycling. In 0.5 mile turn right onto Simonson Road and begin a long descent. At the bottom of the hill take a right onto Valentine's Lane. In about 0.5 mile you will pass the **Louis Clark Nature Refuge**. Though there is no parking area or visitors' center, you will find an extensive freshwater marsh along with all of its customary inhabitants.

Valentine's Lane grows bumpy and narrow as it ends at Northern Boulevard (Route 25A). Although the ride continues to the left (east)

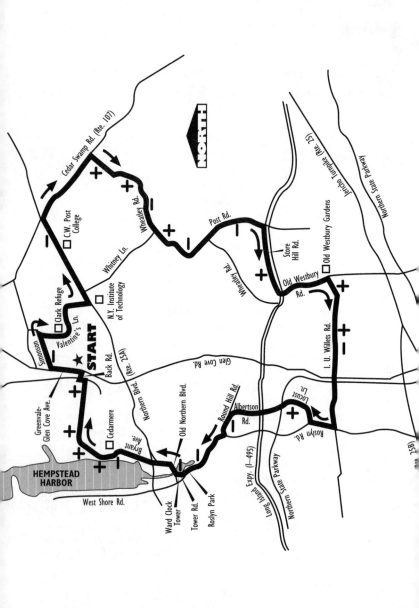

DIREC-TIONS at a glance

0.0	From Greenvale railroad station, head north on Greenvale–Glen Cove Avenue.
0.5	Right onto Simonson Road.
1.0	Right onto Valentine's Lane.
2.0	Left onto Northern Boulevard (Route 25A).
3.1	Right onto Cedar Swamp Road (Route 107).
4.1	Right onto Wheatley Road.
6.5	Straight into Post Road.
7.2	Right onto Store Hill Road.
8.1	Left onto Old Westbury Road.
8.6	Right onto I. U. Willets Road.
10.4	Right onto Roslyn Road.
10.7	Right onto Locust Lane.
11.8	Left onto Round Hill Road.
12.1	Right onto Roslyn Road (later changes to Main Street).
12.9	Right onto Tower Road.
13.0	Right onto Old Northern Boulevard.
13.1	Stay to the left on Old Northern Boulevard.
13.2	Left at fork onto Bryant Avenue.
15.2	Right onto Back Road.
15.3	Right onto Greenvale–Glen Cove Avenue to railroad station.

at this intersection, you might want to take a brief side trip straight into the New **York Institute of Technology**. The terrain of the New York Tech campus is as varied as its curriculum, which ranges from engineering to culinary arts.

Riding eastbound on Northern Boulevard, you will soon pass the entrance to **C. W. Post College**, which was established in 1954 on land donated by Marjorie Meriweather Post. It was subsequently christened C. W. Post in honor of her father, Charles Williams Post, founder of Post Cereals.

Down the hill from the campuses, turn right onto Cedar Swamp Road (Route 107). [If you want to extend your trip into Old Brookville, Sea Cliff, and Glen Cove, turn left here to join Ride #4 from *Short Bike Rides on Long Island.*] In 1 mile take another right and begin to climb Wheatley Road into Brookville. Farther along, as the road rounds a pair of slalomlike turns, watch on the right for the Tudor-style buildings of the Old Westbury Golf and Country Club. You will also coast by a second country club, Glen Oaks Club, after merging with Post Road.

Just before Post crosses under the Long Island Expressway (Interstate 495), turn right onto the westbound service road. Officially labeled Store Hill Road, it does indeed have a hill in store for you—unfortunately, it's one you'll have to pedal up! At the crest turn left onto Old Westbury Road, traversing over the expressway.

Not far down the road, you will come to the imposing, black wrought-iron gates of **Old Westbury Gardens and Mansion.** The seventy-room mansion was built in 1906 by John Phipps, son of Henry Phipps, who was Andrew Carnegie's partner in the Carnegie Steel Company, now known as USX. The grounds, divided into five lovely botanical gardens complete with fountains and pools, are open Wednesday through Sunday from April to October, for a nominal admission charge.

A little farther down Old Westbury Road, turn right onto I. U. Willets Road. Though it begins with a climb, Willets eventually flattens out. After crossing over the Northern State Parkway, take a right at the next traffic light onto Roslyn Road, then a second right onto Locust Lane; both are pleasant roads for cycling. (Note that Locust changes names to Albertson Road as it continues under the Long Island Expressway.) A left at Albertson's end brings you to Round Hill Road. Down the round hill you go, taking a right at its end back onto northbound Roslyn Road.

The road becomes known as Main Street once it enters Roslyn. Charming **Roslyn Park** is there on the right to greet you as you arrive in the village. The park's many wide sidewalks take visitors around the tranquil pond it surrounds. [To extend your trip through Roslyn, take a look at Ride #3 from *Short Bike Rides on Long Island.*]

Roslyn Park marks your entrance into the town's historic district. Along and around narrow Main Street stand no fewer than thirty-seven buildings that date back as far as 1690. It's probably a good idea to get off and walk this part of the route. That way, you won't miss the rich history in the area, but the many cars will miss you!

Turn right onto Tower Road, where you will find the **Ward Clock Tower** at the opposite end. The four-story tower was constructed in 1895 by the children of Ellen Ward (a prominent citizen of Roslyn in the late nineteenth century) as a memorial to their mother.

Back on your bike, make a right onto Old Northern Boulevard, then a left onto Bryant Avenue. Pedal under the Roslyn Viaduct and alongside Hempstead Harbor. The right side of the road, lined with thick woods up a steep bank, is surprisingly rural and seems out of place so close to town. This land is part of the former Bryant estate, **Cedarmere.** In 1843 the celebrated poet William Cullen Bryant purchased two hundred acres of land around Roslyn Harbor, on which he built a farmhouse that came to be known as "Cedarmere." Though largely destroyed by fire twenty-four years after Bryant's death in 1878, the house was redesigned and reconstructed by his grandson. Bequeathed to Nassau County in 1975 by Bryant's great-grandaughter, Cedarmere will eventually open to the public as a museum.

Leaving the harbor behind, Bryant Avenue now winds uphill toward Greenvale. It's a tough climb! Just before Bryant veers to the left, take a quick right onto Back Road. A right onto Greenvale–Glen Cove Avenue brings you back to the Greenvale railroad station.

For Further Information

New York Institute of Technology (516) 686–7516
C. W. Post College (516) 299–0200
Old Westbury Gardens (516) 333–0048

Getting There

The Greenvale railroad station is adjacent to Greenvale–Glen Cove Avenue, about 2 miles north of Exit 39 north on the Long Island Expressway (Interstate 495). For city dwellers who prefer mass transit, the Long Island railroad makes frequent stops here as well.

Suffolk County
Babylon to Islip

Mileage:	25
Approximate pedaling time:	3 hours
Terrain:	Flat
Traffic:	Light to moderate
Things to see:	Argyle Park, Belmont Lake State Park, South Shore Nature Center, Sagtikos Manor, Gardiner County Park, Marconi marker

If you enjoy the open-air freedom of bike riding but tend to shy away because of the hardships associated with hill climbing, then this ride is for you! While the north shore of Long Island contains some of the hilliest territory in the tristate region, the south shore has some of the flattest. On this ride you'll tour portions of Babylon and Islip townships, stopping along the way at several parks. And guess what? No hills! (Well, not many big ones, anyway.)

Begin at **Argyle Park** in the village of Babylon. The park is a wonderful little oasis with a well-manicured lawn surrounding a dammed pond. Three small waterfalls under a quaint pedestrian bridge slowly release the pond's water into a stream that winds toward the Great South Bay.

Head west on Main Street (Route 27A), turning right onto Argyle Avenue just west of the park. Argyle cuts through a pleasant neighborhood of narrow streets and attractive homes. As you snake your way through the surroundings, always stay to the right to remain on Argyle Avenue. Pop out the other side of Argyle and turn left onto Trolley Line Road.

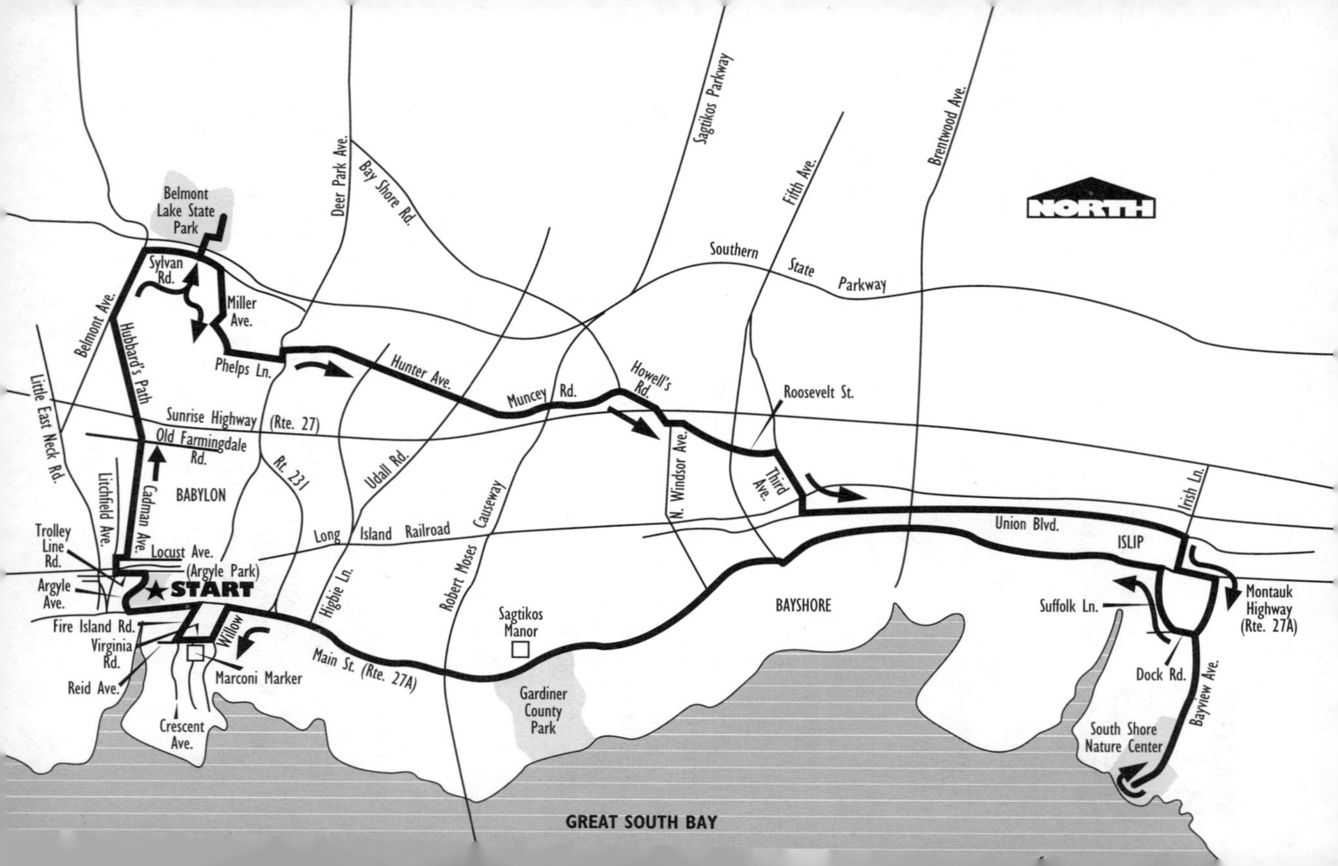
NORTH
Belmont Lake State Park
Sylvan Rd.
Miller Ave.
Belmont Ave.
Hubbard's Path
Phelps Ln.
Deer Park Ave.
Bay Shore Rd.
Sagtikos Parkway
Fifth Ave.
Brentwood Ave.
Southern State Parkway
Hunter Ave.
Muncey Rd.
Howell's Rd.
Roosevelt St.
Little East Neck Rd.
Sunrise Highway (Rte. 27)
Old Farmingdale Rd.
Rt. 231
Udall Rd.
N. Windsor Ave.
Third Ave.
Irish Ln.
Cadman Ave.
BABYLON
Litchfield Ave.
Trolley Line Rd.
Locust Ave.
(Argyle Park)
START
Argyle Ave.
Long Island Railroad
Causeway
Robert Moses
Union Blvd.
ISLIP
Higbie Ln.
Fire Island Rd.
Virginia Rd.
Reid Ave.
Willow
Marconi Marker
Crescent Ave.
Main St. (Rte. 27A)
Sagtikos Manor
Gardiner County Park
BAYSHORE
Suffolk Ln.
Montauk Highway (Rte. 27A)
Dock Rd.
Bayview Ave.
South Shore Nature Center
GREAT SOUTH BAY

0.0 From Argyle Park, head west on Main Street (Route 27A).
0.1 Right on Argyle Avenue.
0.5 Left on Trolley Line Road.
0.6 Right on Litchfield Avenue.
0.7 Right on Locust Avenue.
0.8 Left on Cadman Avenue.
1.7 Left across Old Farmingdale Road onto Hubbard's Path.
2.6 Right on Belmont Avenue.
3.2 Right on Sylvan Road.
3.5 Left into Belmont Lake State Park.
3.7 Right on Miller Avenue (changes ahead to Phelps Lane).
4.8 Left onto Deer Park Avenue.
4.9 Right onto Hunter Avenue (changes to Muncey Road after crossing Udall Road in Islip).
7.4 Right onto Howell's Road.
7.9 Right to stay on Howell's Road.
8.5 Follow road to left onto Roosevelt Street.
8.7 Follow road to right onto Third Avenue.
9.3 Left onto Union Boulevard.
12.1 Right onto Irish Lane.
12.4 Left onto Montauk Highway.
12.6 Right on Bayview Avenue.
13.4 Right into South Shore Nature Center or straight to East Islip Marina—turn around.
15.6 Left on Dock Road.
15.7 Right onto unmarked Suffolk Lane.
16.2 Left onto Montauk Highway (Route 27A).
23.5 Left onto Willow Street.
23.7 Right onto Virginia Road.
23.9 Straight on Fire Island Road.
24.0 Right to continue on Fire Island Road.
24.3 Left onto Main Street (Route 27A).
24.5 Back at Argyle Park.

After a short westward trek, bear right onto Litchfield Avenue and cross under the railroad bridge. At the first stop sign, turn right onto Locust Avenue, followed by a left onto Cadman Avenue. At its end jog to the left across Old Farmingdale Road and onto Hubbard's Path. Hubbard's Path slices diagonally northwest to Belmont Avenue, where you turn right. Just before Belmont crosses the Southern State Parkway, take another right, this time onto Sylvan Road.

Follow the signs on Sylvan toward the main entrance of **Belmont Lake State Park.** This 459-acre park is built on part of the former estate of financier and avid horseman August Belmont. The original estate was built on 1,100 acres, half of which was pastureland for Belmont's horses and livestock. His twenty-four–room mansion, once the pinnacle of Long Island high society, now houses the Long Island State Park and Recreation Commission's headquarters. The state park offers picnic and play areas, rowboat rentals and fishing on forty-acre Belmont Lake, trails for bicycles, hikers, and horses, ball fields, restrooms, and a refreshment stand.

Exit the park as you entered it and continue east on Sylvan Road for 0.1 mile; then steer right onto Miller Avenue. Not long after Miller makes a sharp left and changes names to Phelps Lane, you will pass another picturesque body of water, Elda Lake.

Phelps Lane ends at Deer Park Avenue. If you wish to return to Babylon at this point, turn right on Deer Park; otherwise, make a quick turn to the left, then another to the right to end up on Hunter Avenue bound for Islip. Follow Hunter as it changes names to Muncey Road after crossing Udall Road. At its end turn right onto Howell's Road. Following Howell's is a bit confusing on the other side of Sunrise Highway; be careful not to miss the right-hand turn as it veers off of the highway's service road.

Follow Howell's as it snakes to the left, merging into Roosevelt Street, then winds to the right into Third Avenue. After crossing under the railroad bridge, turn left onto Union Boulevard and continue toward the east. Union, a moderately crowded four-lane thoroughfare, has no real shoulder for cycling and should be approached with caution. If this concerns you, continue on Third Avenue to Montauk Highway (Route 27A) and head east, picking up the ride at

Bayview Avenue. (If you want a shortcut back home at this juncture, take Montauk Highway westbound instead.)

After passing Knapps Lake take the next right onto Irish Lane. At its end continue to the left onto eastbound Montauk Highway, followed by a right onto Bayview Avenue. Bayview offers a long, flat ride out toward the water's edge, where you will find the entrance to the South Shore Nature Center on the right and the East Islip Marina all the way at the road's bumpy end.

The **South Shore Nature Center,** open year-round, features a nature museum and 2 miles of hiking trails. These trails meander through eight different environments, ranging from forests to freshwater and saltwater marshes. There is no admission charge to enter the nature center; souvenirs and trail guidebooks are available at nominal fees.

For a little change of pace, return to Montauk Highway on Dock Road and Suffolk Lane. Then take one more left onto Montauk Highway (Route 27A west) for the 8-mile return trip to Babylon. [If you wish to lengthen your excursion, continue east on Montauk Highway, where you may join Ride #20 from *Short Bike Rides on Long Island* for a jaunt through Oakdale.]

On the way back to Babylon, watch for the large white sign pointing to **Sagtikos Manor.** The original manor was built in 1697 by Stephanus Van Cortlandt on a 1,200-acre plot of land he purchased from the Secatogue Indians. Van Cortlandt named his estate *Sagtikos,* an Indian word meaning "snake that hisses." Since 1758 the estate has been owned by the Gardiner family, who enlarged it to its present size in the late 1800s. And yes, George Washington *did* sleep here (it was during his 1790 tour of Long Island). The manor is open to visitors from Memorial Day to Labor Day. While only ten acres from the original Van Cortlandt estate remain with the home today, they contain lovely gardens and a family cemetery.

Across Montauk Highway from the manor entrance is **Gardiner County Park,** which features a nature center and trails that pass through open fields, woods, and marshland. If you have a little extra time and energy, lock your bike and join one of the guided nature walks that are offered regularly.

Just after maneuvering through the intersection with Route 231, turn left onto Willow Street. In three short blocks, take a right on Virginia Road. The other end of Virginia Road, where it meets Fire Island Road, is famous in the annals of history. As the historical **Marconi marker** on the left reads, this was "the site of the birth of American wireless. A pioneer station here in 1901 first talked to ships at sea." That radio station, set up and operated by Guglielmo Marconi, ushered in the age of electronic communications.

From here it's a quick ride to the north end of Fire Island Road. A left turn onto Main Street brings you back to Argyle Park and the ride's departure point.

For Further Information

Belmont Lake State Park (516) 667–5055
South Shore Nature Center (516) 224–5436
Sagtikos Manor (516) 661–0137
Gardiner County Park (516) 666–5333

Getting There

Argyle Park is just west of Babylon village on Main Street (also known as Montauk Highway or Route 27A). Take Exit 39 south from the Southern State Parkway or Exit RM2 west from the Robert Moses Causeway. Parking is available in the park. For mass-transit riders, the Long Island Railroad's Babylon station is on the corner of Deer Park Avenue and Trolley Line Road.

Suffolk County
Smithtown

Mileage:	23
Approximate pedaling time:	3 hours
Terrain:	Hilly
Traffic:	Moderate on Route 25, light elsewhere
Things to see:	Smithtown Historical District, Kings Park Bluff, Sunken Meadow State Park, Smithtown Bull, Blydenburgh County Park

Surrounding the Nissequogue River on the north shore of western Suffolk County is the village of Smithtown. Smithtown exemplifies much of modern-day Long Island—a nice blend of contemporary and historical flavors nestled in a pleasant suburban setting.

Just east of the town's center (also known as the Village of the Branch) on the north side of Main Street (Route 25) are a number of buildings that date back to the town's beginnings. Among the buildings found in the **Smithtown Historical District** are the Caleb Smith House (1819), open daily except Sundays and featuring historic exhibits; the Epenetus Smith Tavern (1740); the J. Lawrence Smith Homestead (circa 1750); and the Franklin Arthur Farm (1740), complete with carriage house, barn, and smokehouse. All are maintained by the Smithtown Historical Society.

Our route heads out of the Village of the Branch on Landing Avenue. The town's bustling commercial center quickly gives way to a quiet tree-lined street of stately homes. Crossing Edgewood Avenue the route plunges toward its first crossing of the Nissequogue. On the right is Landing Avenue Park, featuring a playground and a small pic-

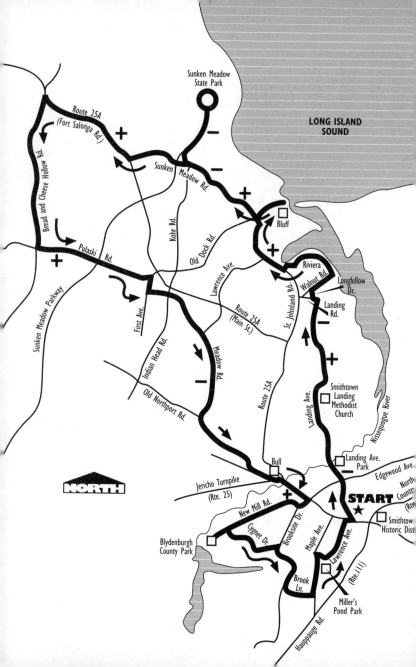

DIREC- TIONS at a glance

0.0	From town center head north on Landing Avenue.
2.9	Left onto Landing Road.
3.0	Right onto Longfellow Drive.
3.1	Right onto Walnut Road.
3.4	Left onto Riviera Drive.

4.0 At fork, keep right on Riviera.

4.3 Right onto Saint Johnland Road.

5.2 Right onto Old Dock Road, continuing to its end. Turn around, returning to the Saint Johnland/Sunken Meadow Road intersection. Right onto Sunken Meadow Road.

7.3 Right through gate into Sunken Meadow Park.

8.3 Exit park back through gate. Continue right (west) on Sunken Meadow Road.

9.0 Right onto Fort Salonga Road (Route 25A).

10.8 Left onto Bread and Cheese Hollow Road.

12.9 Left onto Pulaski Road.

14.4 Right onto First Avenue.

14.6 Left onto Meadow Road.

16.6 Left at flashing light to continue on Meadow Road.

17.6 Left at traffic light to stay on Meadow Road.

18.0 Left onto Jericho Turnpike (Route 25).

18.5 Right onto Brooksite Drive.

18.7 Right onto New Mill Road.

19.9 Straight into Blydenburgh Park. Exit through same gate back onto New Mill Road.

20.2 Right onto Cygnet Drive.

21.0 Right onto Brooksite Drive.

21.6 Left onto Brook Lane.

22.1 Left onto Maple Avenue.

22.6 Right onto Lawrence Avenue.

23.3 Right onto Main Street (Route 25).

nic area. It is not unusual to spot a canoe or a kayak maneuvering downriver, especially on warmer weekends.

Farther down Landing Avenue on the right, just before the ride's first big climb, is the Smithtown Landing Methodist Church. Wandering through the churchyard, you will find stones dating back to the 1830s. Though not used for weekly services, the church still hosts special gatherings.

Continuing northward the road climbs until it crests at the Smithtown Landing Country Club. Open to town residents only, the club boasts a fine golf course, a clubhouse, and three outdoor pools.

As quickly as it rose, Landing Avenue drops toward its northern end, where the ride takes a left and two rights to end up on Riviera Drive. You will soon find yourself riding along the western shore of the Nissequogue's mouth, a lovely example of a saltwater marshland populated by many different waterfowl.

Turn right onto Saint Johnland Road, where you will shortly pass the Obediah Smith House on the right. Constructed in 1700, it was the home of a grandson of the town's founder and is now preserved by the town's historical society. [If you wish to return to Smithtown, turn left onto Saint Johnland. Continue straight onto Route 25A, then follow it east into Smithtown.]

Continue to the first traffic light; then turn right onto Old Dock Road. At its end lies the **Kings Park Bluff**, a favorite haven for weekend mariners. Across the bay you can spot Short Beach and, in the distance, the Connecticut shore. For lunch, the Old Dock Inn offers elegant seafood dining.

Return to Saint Johnland and turn right. Now called Sunken Meadow Road, the route takes on a roller-coaster-like profile with many ups and downs. Just before the road crosses under a stone bridge, dismount and enter **Sunken Meadow State Park** through the pedestrian gate on the right. Located on Long Island Sound, the park is best known for its mile-long beach and boardwalk. Also found within its 1,266 acres are numerous picnic areas, playgrounds, and hiking trails. After you have explored the park, exit as you entered and continue down Sunken Meadow Road to Fort Salonga Road (Route 25A).

As you approach the Fort Salonga Shopping Center (where there are restaurants, a deli, and a supermarket), turn left onto Bread and Cheese Hollow Road. A flat run, Bread and Cheese Hollow winds along the Smithtown-Huntington town line, wedged between two ridges. At its end take a left onto Pulaski Road for an uphill battle into the Kings Park section of Smithtown.

Exit Kings Park on Meadow Road, a (mostly) downhill trek that leads all the way to Jericho Turnpike (Route 25). After turning left to join Jericho and passing under the Long Island Railroad trestle, watch out for the **bull** on the left. A bull? That's right, but it's not a real bull; rather it's a statue commemorating Smithtown's founding in 1665. According to legend, local Indians agreed to sell Richard Smythe, the town's founder, as much land as he could circle in one day while riding a bull. Smythe supposedly set out on his bull Whisper on the day of the summer solstice, completing a 35-mile journey by nightfall. Historians debate the accuracy of this tale, but the statue of Whisper has nevertheless become a county landmark.

Stay on Jericho to the top of the next hill; then take a quick right onto Brooksite Drive and another onto New Mill Road. New Mill, which passes through a serene neighborhood of homes, offers one of the nicest cycling environments on the entire ride. Follow it all the way to its end to enter **Blydenburgh County Park**. Inside, many hiking trails, playgrounds, and picnic areas surround Stump Pond, a beautiful body of water. The pond was created at the turn of the century when residents dammed the Nissequogue River using tree stumps (hence the name). Rental boats are available, as are a limited number of campsites. If you have never tried bicycle camping before, here is the perfect chance. Pack as light as possible (hiking gear is a must) and enjoy!

The ride concludes by zigzagging through other tranquil residential neighborhoods. You may want to make a last stop at Miller's Pond Park, located on Maple Avenue. The pond is usually swarming with ducks, geese, and swans, all eagerly vying for the bread thrown by visiting children and parents. From the park take a right onto Lawrence Avenue for the final sprint back into the town center. If you are up to it, you can link up with Ride #9 from *Short Bike Rides on*

Long Island by continuing east on Main Street (Route 25) to the intersection with North Country Road (Route 25A).

For Further Information

Smithtown Historical Society (516) 265–6768
Sunken Meadow State Park (516) 269–4333
Blydenburgh County Park (516) 360–4966

Getting There

Smithtown is easily reached via the Long Island Expressway (take Exit 56 north) or the Northern State Parkway (take it to its end, then follow Route 347 to Route 111 north). Trains along the Long Island Railroad's Port Jefferson line make frequent stops at both the Smithtown and Kings Park stations.

Westchester County
Harrison to Rye

Mileage:	16
Approximate pedaling time:	2 hours
Terrain:	Hilly in spots
Traffic:	Light to moderate
Things to see:	Station Park, Haviland Family Cemetery, Westchester Country Club, Rye Nature Center, Playland

Though the two towns coexist peacefully today, the early ties between Harrison and Rye were anything but tranquil. The trouble started in 1662, when four settlers purchased much of the area from the Siwanoy Indians. Unfortunately, the settlers failed to apply for a patent; as a result, their claim was never officially sanctioned by the provincial government. In 1695 part of the same land was sold to John Harrison, who had the land surveyed by the British government and was subsequently granted a patent. With tempers flaring over this series of events, Rye temporarily seceded from New York. Though the wounds soon healed, the distinction between the towns remained vague until 1788, when the county finally recognized Harrison as a separate township.

Begin your tour of the towns at **Station Park,** adjacent to the Harrison railroad station at the corner of Heineman Place and Harrison Avenue (Route 127). Begin by heading north on Harrison Avenue. In about a mile turn left onto Sterling Road, followed by another left at the fork onto Woodlands Road. Both take you through a lovely neighborhood of attractive homes. Stay to the left at each of the stop signs that you will meet along the way.

Woodlands Road ends at Pleasant Ridge Road, where the ride

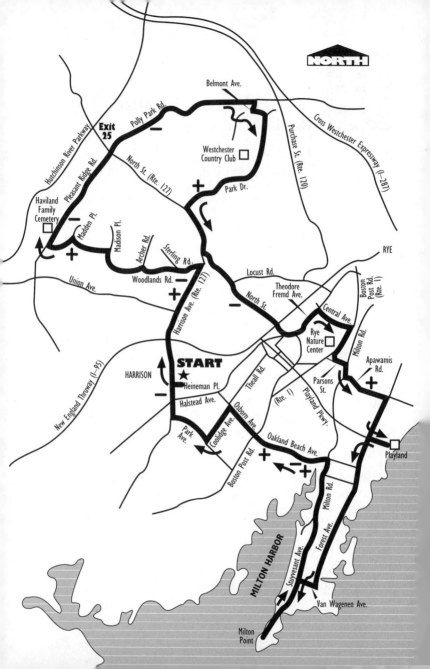

0.0   Begin at Station Park at the corner of Harrison Avenue (Route 127) and Heineman Place. North on Harrison.

1.1   Left onto Sterling Road.

1.2   Left onto Woodlands Road.

2.0   Left at stop sign to stay on Woodlands Road.

2.3   Left again at stop sign to stay on Woodlands Road.

2.6   Right onto Pleasant Ridge Road.

3.5   Straight across North Street (Route 127) onto Polly Park Road.

5.0   Right onto Belmont Avenue.

5.1   Left to stay on Belmont Avenue.

5.2   Right onto Park Drive.

6.5   Left onto North Street (Route 127).

7.0   Left at traffic light to stay on North Street.

8.0   Left onto Theodore Fremd Avenue.

8.4   Right onto Central Avenue.

8.7   Right onto Boston Post Road (Route 1).

9.0   Left onto Parsons Street.

9.2   Right onto Milton Road.

9.3   Left onto Apawamis Road.

9.7   Right onto Forest Avenue.

11.3   Right onto Van Wagenen Avenue.

11.5   Left onto Stuyvesant Avenue.

12.0   Turn around at end of Stuyvesant Avenue.

13.1   Right onto Milton Road.

13.5   Left onto Oakland Beach Avenue.

14.5   Left onto Coolidge Avenue.

14.9   Right onto Park Avenue.

15.1   Right onto Harrison Avenue (Route 127).

15.6   Back at Station Park.

turns right. Not too far down on the left side of Pleasant Ridge, watch for a small family cemetery set back from the road. This is the **Haviland Family Cemetery**, and it contains several dozen headstones dating back to the early 1800s.

Continue straight across the intersection with North Street (Route 127) onto Polly Park Road. Polly Park is a challenging road, not so much for the hills (though there are a few) as for its rutted surface. Be careful.

Just before Polly Park meets Purchase Street, turn right on Belmont Avenue and enter the posh world of the **Westchester Country Club.** Circle around the club's immaculate grounds by taking Belmont around to the left, followed by a right onto Park Drive. Originally known as the Westchester Biltmore, the country club opened in 1922 on the site of the former Hobart Park Farm. Designed by John Bowman, the club became an instant world-class showpiece thanks to its huge clubhouse, three golf courses, polo field, and tennis and squash courts. Half a century later it remains one of the premier examples of opulent living and is perhaps best known as the site of the annual Westchester Open professional golf tournament. The regal flavor continues to the end of Park Drive as you pedal pass some truly elegant homes set on immaculately manicured lawns.

Turn left and head south on North Street (Route 127). After passing St. Vincent's Hospital, turn left at the traffic light to continue along North Street. [For a quick return to the starting point, follow Route 127 south to Station Park.] Soon you will pass the Willow Ridge Golf Club on the left and Greenwood Union Cemetery on the right. Coasting past the cemetery, you will cross the town line of Harrison and enter neighboring Rye.

After riding up and over the railroad tracks and the New England Thruway (Interstate 95), turn left onto Theodore Fremd Avenue. This is followed by a right in 0.4 mile onto Central Avenue. Another right at its end puts you on the Boston Post Road (Route 1) westbound.

For the next 0.25 mile the road parallels a small woodland strip on the right. Within, an unpaved footpath follows Blind Brook as both approach the main entrance to **Rye Nature Center.** Turn into the center's entrance road and continue up and along to the visitors' center.

The nature center is located on the grounds of the former estate of financier Marselis Parsons. In 1906 Parsons built a huge mansion that must surely have been the talk of the town. Then came the Stock Market crash of 1929, and Parsons lost most of his fortune. Adding to the family's losses was a fire of "mysterious origin" that leveled the mansion in 1942. All that remains of this grand home is its massive stone foundation with two chimneys towering above. Three years after the fire, the town of Rye purchased thirty-five acres of the estate; an additional twelve were acquired between 1959 and 1964.

Today the Rye Nature Center features a museum, a solar greenhouse, a research laboratory, and more than 2.5 miles of hiking trails. These trails meander through open fields and dense forests and past pond and stream environments. A self-guided interpretive tour helps visitors learn about the more than 70 different species of trees, 125 types of wildflowers, and more than 180 species of birds that inhabit the woods. The center is open daily, though the museum is closed on Sundays. There is no charge for admission.

Exiting the center, turn left on Parsons Street, followed by a right onto Milton Road, a left onto Apawamis Road, and finally a right onto Forest Avenue. In 0.25 mile you will pass an intersection with Playland Parkway, where a left will take you to **Rye Beach and Playland Amusement Park.** When it opened in 1928, Playland was one of the nation's first planned amusement parks. Since then it has grown to include more than fifty rides, a horseshoe-shaped beach and boardwalk, and a large saltwater lake. Playland is noted among amusement-park connoisseurs for its wooden "Dragon Coaster" and vintage merry-go-round, while students of architecture enjoy the art deco buildings found along the grassy central mall. Though there is no admission charge into the park itself, tickets are required for the amusements. Park hours vary by season so it's best to call before you visit.

Proceed to the end of Forest. Turn right onto Van Wagenen Avenue and left onto Stuyvesant Avenue. Stuyvesant continues past several ritzy yacht clubs on its way toward the tip of Milton Point.

When you can't go any farther, turn around to begin the journey back home. Follow Stuyvesant to Milton Road; then turn left onto Oakland Beach Avenue. After crossing the Boston Post Road (Route

1), the road changes names to Osborn Avenue. As Osborn heads downhill turn left onto Coolidge Avenue. Two right turns, one onto Park Avenue and another onto Harrison Avenue (Route 127) bring you back into the center of Harrison. One final climb over the railroad tracks returns you to Station Park.

For Further Information

Westchester Country Club (914) 967–6000
Rye Nature Center (914) 967–5150
Playland (914) 967–2040

Getting There

The center of Harrison is easily accessible from either Exit 19 off the New England Thruway (Interstate 95) or Exit 25 off the Hutchinson River Parkway (Route 15). For mass-transit travelers, Metro North's New Haven line stops regularly at the Harrison railroad station.

Westchester County
Kensico Reservoir Loop

Mileage:	15
Approximate pedaling time:	2 hours
Terrain:	Hilly
Traffic:	Light
Things to see:	Kensico Reservoir, Kensico Dam Plaza, Cranberry Lake Park

Of the many reservoirs and lakes scattered throughout upper Westchester County, none is more beautiful than **Kensico Reservoir**. The reservoir is situated in a long, slender valley surrounded by hills on three sides and Kensico Dam on the fourth. The dam began as an earthen embankment in 1885. It was subsequently enlarged to its present size by 1917, to provide more drinking water to a thirsty New York City.

Begin your circuit of Kensico Reservoir from the park at the base of Kensico Dam. **Kensico Dam Plaza** features many paved trails around the base of the dam, providing hours of fascination for nature lovers. In addition, the plaza, maintained by the Westchester County Department of Parks, hosts outdoor concerts and other activities during the warmer months.

Take a right turn out of Kensico Plaza onto Broadway in Valhalla and get ready to scale the height of the dam as you turn right onto North Kensico Avenue. The road travels, in effect, from the base of the dam to the shore of the reservoir in only 0.2 mile. Its rutted concrete surface only adds to the difficulty of the climb; most readers probably will do best by dismounting their bikes and walking its length.

Once at the end of North Kensico Avenue, turn left onto West

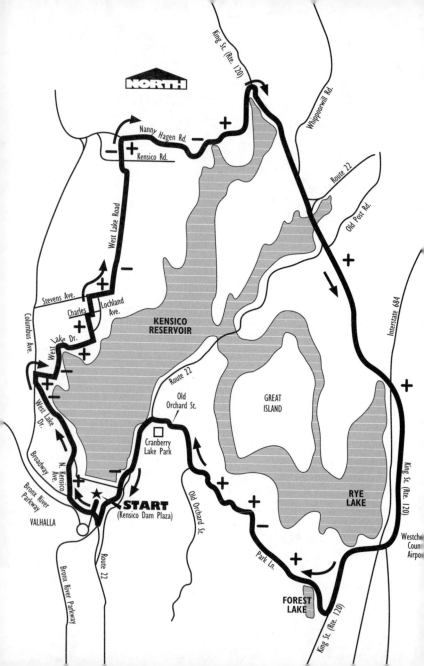

NORTH

King St. (Rte. 120)

Whippoorwill Rd.

Nanny Hagen Rd.

Kensico Rd.

West Lake Road

Route 22

Old Post Rd.

Stevens Ave.

Charles

Lochland Ave.

Columbus Ave.

West Lake Dr.

KENSICO RESERVOIR

Interstate 684

Route 22

Old Orchard St.

GREAT ISLAND

West Lake Dr.

Cranberry Lake Park

King St. (Rte. 120)

Broadway

N. Kensico Ave.

Old Orchard St.

RYE LAKE

Bronx River Parkway

START
(Kensico Dam Plaza)

VALHALLA

Route 22

Park Ln.

Westchester County Airport

Bronx River Parkway

FOREST LAKE

King St. (Rte. 120)

DIREC- TIONS at a glance

0.0	Leave Kensico Dam Plaza and turn right onto Broadway.
0.5	Right onto North Kensico Avenue.
0.7	Left onto West Lake Drive.
1.6	Right onto Columbus Avenue.
1.7	Right onto West Lake Drive.
2.5	Left to follow West Lake Drive.
2.7	Right to stay on West Lake Drive (Charles Street enters on left).
2.8	Left to follow West Lake Drive (Lochland Avenue continues straight).
2.9	Right to stay on West Lake Drive (Stevens Avenue enters on left).
4.5	Right onto Nanny Hagen Road.
6.1	Right onto King Street (Route 120).
7.6	Left at traffic light to follow Route 120.
11.0	Right onto Park Lane.
12.7	Continue diagonally right onto Old Orchard Street.
13.4	Left onto Route 22.
14.1	Right toward Bronx and Taconic parkways.
14.7	Right at stop sign onto Broadway.
14.8	Straight into Kensico Plaza.

Lake Drive and enjoy the view! Kensico Reservoir covers 13.3 square miles and holds more than 30 billion gallons of water. Direct public access to its shore is strictly limited in an effort to minimize possible pollution.

West Lake Drive ends at the intersection with Columbus Avenue. Or does it? Take a right onto Columbus, followed by another right just down the road back onto West Lake Drive. After passing a reservoir maintenance complex, West Lake Drive takes on a wooded, rural personality and is free of heavy traffic. Though it has its ups and downs, you will enjoy the scenic ride. All along, watch as the reservoir peeks through the trees on the right. An especially lovely view is found as the road bends sharply to the right around a deep crevice in the land.

Civilization returns as West Lake Drive begins to ascend. Follow the accompanying map carefully, zigging to the left and zagging to the right as indicated. As the road straightens out, enjoy a long, slow downhill coast toward the campus of West Lake High School and the village of Thornwood.

Stay on West Lake Drive as it veers around a monstrous green water tank and continues all the way to its end at Nanny Hagen Road. A right at this juncture takes you back toward Kensico Reservoir and its enclosing wilderness. In about a mile the road takes a sharp right. Off to the right the view of the water is truly outstanding; just be careful around that curve—it's a long way down!

Nanny Hagen Road continues to play hide-and-seek with the reservoir until it ends at King Street (Route 120). Though busier than Nanny Hagen Road, King Street is a pleasant highway for cycling thanks to a broad, smooth shoulder. (The only point of concern should be where Route 22 joins in from the left; the traffic there can be a bit harrowing.)

Continue to the left on Route 120 South as Route 22 peels off to the right. (If you want to return to Kensico Plaza more quickly, stay on Route 22, which meets up with the ride at Old Orchard Street in 1.8 miles. But be forewarned: the route is both hilly and narrow in spots.) Though it opens with a narrow, uphill run itself, Route 120 quickly opens up and flattens out as it nears the New York–Connecticut state line. A bit farther along it wedges between Westchester County Airport, on the other side of the hills to the left, and an extension of Kensico Reservoir known as Rye Lake on the right.

After crossing over Interstate 684 a second time, take the next right onto Park Lane. Although the road sign is easy to miss, you should have no trouble spotting the sign for the Hillside Farm Nursery. After joining Park the route meanders past Forest Lake, a small body of water surrounded by unspoiled woodlands. Park is a bit on the narrow and windy side, but the light traffic makes it an acceptable challenge for cycling.

Park ends at a stop sign, with your route jogging to the right onto Old Orchard Street. Bordering the road to the left is **Cranberry Lake Park.** It was from here that the stones for Kensico Dam were exhumed and transported by a special rail line in 1915. Today Cranberry Park contains miles of hiking trails for nature lovers to enjoy. Bicycles may be locked near the park's ranger station.

About 0.7 mile after joining Route 22 for your final sprint back to Kensico Plaza, be on the lookout for a sign pointing toward the Bronx and Taconic parkways. Take that road as it plunges off of Route 22 and down toward Broadway. (You will know you missed this turnoff if you come to the intersection with West Lake Drive; carefully turn around and try again.) At the bottom of the hill, turn right onto Broadway and continue straight back into Kensico Dam Plaza.

The Bronx River Parkway is closed to automobiles from 10 A.M. to 2 P.M. every Sunday from May through September (except holiday weekends) for "Bicycle Sunday." Cyclists can ride worry-free on these days from the County Center in White Plains to Scarsdale Road in Yonkers, a 14-mile round-trip.

For Further Information

Elijah Miller House (914) 949–1236
Bicycle Sunday (914) 285–PARK

Getting There

Kensico Dam Plaza is directly accessible from Exit 27 (Broadway) on the Bronx River Parkway. For those who prefer mass transit, Metro North's Harlem division stops in Valhalla. The station is just north of the plaza.

Westchester County
Bedford and Vicinity

Mileage:	17
Approximate pedaling time:	3 hours
Terrain:	Hilly, with some dirt roads
Traffic:	Light
Things to see:	Bedford Historic Village Green, Sutton Clock Tower, Byram Lake, Middle Patent Rural Cemetery, Mianus River Gorge Wildlife Refuge

Located in the picturesque surroundings of mid-Westchester County, Bedford represents the quintessential small town. The village is built around a large, tree-lined **green** and is comprised of a number of small stores (including a highly recommended delicatessen) and historical buildings that you may want to visit.

The town green is a favorite starting point among local cyclists for many adventures. This ride passes several historic and natural landmarks while covering a wide variety of local roads. Before embarking, note that you will pass over several short stretches of dirt road. While quite well maintained by the highway department, they require extra care on the part of the rider.

From the village center head north for a short distance on Cantitoe Road (Route 22). Just over a rise beyond town, as Cantitoe Road veers to the right, take a left-hand turn onto Guard Hill Road. Guard Hill Road is rich in colonial history, as it was one of the first routes cleared by early area settlers.

As you approach the intersection with Clinton Road, Guard Hill begins to alternate between a paved and dirt surface. Though actually smoother than some paved roads in the area, the dirt sections should

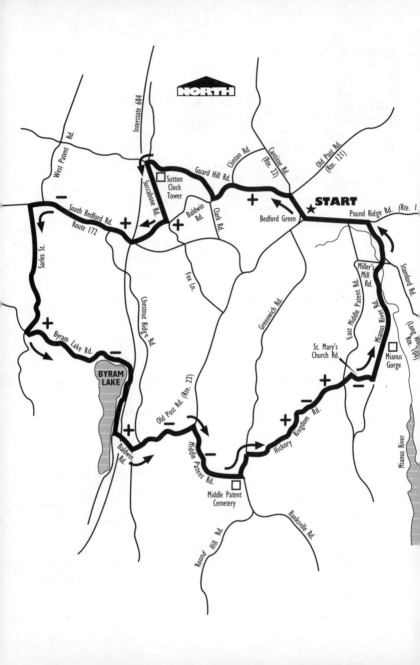

DIREC-TIONS
at a glance

0.0 Head north on Cantitoe Road (Route 22).
0.3 Left onto Guard Hill Road.
2.4 Left onto Succabone Road.
3.1 Right onto Baldwin Road.
3.7 Right onto South Bedford Road (Route 172).
5.5 Left onto Sarles Street.
7.0 Left onto Byram Lake Road.
9.4 Left onto unmarked Baldwin Road.
9.8 Left onto Old Post Road (Route 22).
10.6 Right onto Middle Patent Road.
11.6 Left onto Greenwich Road.
12.0 Right onto Hickory Kingdom Road.
13.8 At Saint Mary's Church, continue straight onto Saint Mary's Church Road.
14.3 Left onto Mianus River Road.
15.8 Right onto Miller's Mill Road, then left after crossing river.
15.9 Left onto Stamford Road (Route 104).
16.5 Left onto Pound Ridge Road (Route 172).
17.3 At the village green, bear right back into Bedford.

be navigated slowly, especially after a recent rain. Fortunately, most of the uphill portions are paved.

At the intersection of Guard Hill and Succabone roads is a famous local landmark, the **Sutton Clock Tower.** Erected in 1939, the tower houses a fine, century-old clock complete with a 550-pound bell. The clock was originally installed in the barn of local residents Mr. and Mrs. James Sutton. Although the barn burned in 1929, the clock and bell were saved and, a decade later, were installed in the current tower after a group of Bedford citizens raised funds for its construction. The clock continues to be maintained by the Bedford Historical Society and is wound weekly by its neighbors.

At the clock turn left onto Succabone Road. For the next few miles, as you go from Succabone to Baldwin Road and South Bedford Road (Route 172), you are faced with a mostly uphill run. The pain of the hills is tempered somewhat by their scenic beauty, thanks to some woods, fields, and an occasional barn. You finally reach the hill's summit about a mile after joining South Bedford Road, only to head quickly back down. Take care not to build up too much speed, as it is easy to flash past your next left-hand turn onto Sarles Street.

Follow Sarles for about 1.5 miles to a four-way intersection with Byram Lake Road, where the route again turns left. Approaching the lake itself, the road slopes steeply downward and is especially narrow and curvy. With the pavement giving way to a hard dirt surface, the route travels along the north and east shores of **Byram Lake**. The lake is outstanding for its natural beauty, especially in the autumn, and makes an ideal midway stopping point for an impromptu roadside picnic.

Your next turn, onto Baldwin Road, is unmarked but is easily identifiable as a short uphill run passing under Interstate 684 and ending at Old Post Road (Route 22). At the intersection with Old Post Road, begin a long and refreshing downhill trek that glides all the way to the end of Middle Patent Road, where you will find the **Middle Patent Rural Cemetery**, on the corner of Middle Patent Road and Greenwich Road. Established in 1743, this colonial cemetery holds the graves of fifteen Revolutionary War soldiers. Just beyond the opposite corner is the Middle Patent Methodist/Episcopal Church, built in 1825.

The ride continues to the right on Greenwich Road for a short distance, then right again onto Hickory Kingdom Road. The latter crosses some of the hilliest terrain on the entire route and may well require riders to dismount and walk a bit. [To shorten the ride, follow Greenwich Road all the way to its end, then turn right on Route 22 back into Bedford.]

Continue as straight as possible through the confusing intersection with East Middle Patent Road. The journey curves around and behind Saint Mary's Episcopal Church (built in 1851), zigzagging down a steep hill and onto narrow Saint Mary's Church Road.

Turning left onto Mianus River Road, you again travel along a serene, little-used thoroughfare. About halfway down the road lies the **Mianus River Gorge Wildlife Refuge**. For those who have a little extra energy, many enjoyable hours may be spent exploring this unique, untouched haven. Beginning at the small visitors' shelter, three footpaths of varying lengths (1 mile, 2 miles, and 5 miles) allow hikers to explore the flora and fauna of this beautiful gorge. We personally recommend taking the longer "C" trail, which takes explorers past three-hundred-year-old hemlocks, an eighteenth-century mica quarry, and picturesque Havemeyer Falls.

As Mianus River Road continues, the pavement once again alternates between finished and unfinished surfaces. Bearing right at the road's end onto Miller's Mill Road, continue over the small bridge and then turn left past Miller's Mill itself. Follow Stamford Road (Route 104) north, then Pound Ridge Road (Route 172) west into Bedford and the village green starting point.

For Further Information

Bedford Historical Society (914) 234–9328
Mianus River Gorge Refuge (914) 234–3455

Getting There

The village of Bedford is most easily reached by taking Exit 4 off Interstate 684 onto Route 172. Proceed east for 2 miles to Route 22; follow 22 north into town. For rail riders, take Metro North to the Bedford Hills station. From there, follow Bedford Center Road east for 3 miles; then turn right onto Route 22. Follow 22 for about a mile into Bedford Village. (If you wish, you may turn right at Succabone Road and join the ride at its intersection with Guard Hill Road about 2 miles later.)

Westchester County
Katonah and Croton Reservoir

Mileage:	33
Approximate pedaling time:	4 hours
Terrain:	Hilly
Traffic:	Light
Things to see:	Croton Reservoir, Muscoot Farm, Croton Gorge Park, Teatown Lake Reservation, Elephant Hotel (optional)

A century ago the town of Katonah was much different—and much drier—than it is today. In 1894 town officials were informed of a decision made by the New York City Board of Water Supply to flood most of Katonah's lowlands to create a vast reservoir. Facing a crisis that would change the village for all generations to come, the town board voted to move most of the affected homes to new, higher plots of land. This meant lifting each structure off its foundation, towing it by horses over timber tracks to a new site, and then securing it to a new substructure.

A second project authorized by the town board created a new, grand village center. Bedford Road was widened to 100 feet across. Opposing one-way wagon paths were separated by a grassy strip planted with trees and flowers. Although the wagon paths have since been paved for modern horseless carriages, Bedford Road (now known as Route 117) retains its century-old charm.

Lining the road are many charming buildings from that long-ago era. One of the finest is the Methodist-Episcopal Church, which features cobblestoned floors and an open belfry. For art lovers the Katonah Gallery, located at the rear of the Katonah Public Library, has

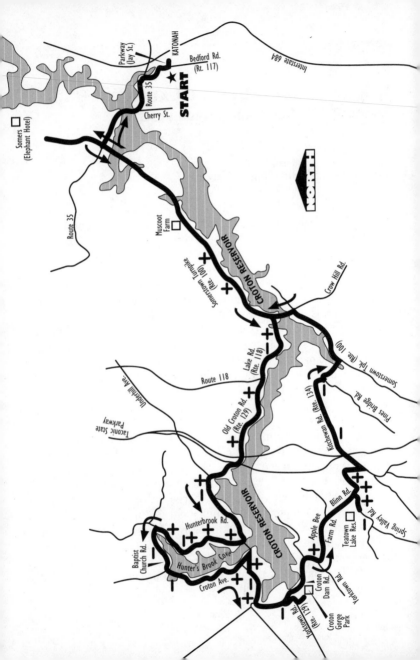

KATONAH

Parkway (Jay St.)

Bedford Rd. (Rt. 117)

Interstate 684

Route 35

★ START

Cherry St.

Somers (Elephant Hotel)

Route 35

NORTH

Muscoot Farm

Somerstown Turnpike (Rte. 100)

CROTON RESERVOIR

Crow Hill Rd.

Lake Rd. (Rte. 118)

Somerstown Tpk. (Rte. 100)

Route 118

Underhill Ave.

Old Croton Rd. (Rte. 129)

Taconic State Parkway

Kitchawan Rd. (Rte. 134)

Pines Bridge Rd.

Hunterbrook Rd.

Apple Bee Farm Rd.

Blinn Rd.

Spring Valley Rd.

Teatown Lake Res.

Baptist Church Rd.

Hunter's Brook Cove

Croton Ave.

CROTON RESERVOIR

Yorktown Rd.

Croton Dam Rd.

Croton Gorge Park

Yorktown Rd. (Rte. 129)

0.0	Right at the corner of the Parkway and Bedford Road (Route 117).
0.5	Left onto Route 35 west.
1.9	Left onto Somerstown Turnpike (Route 100 south).
6.4	Right onto Lake Road (Route 118 north).
7.6	Straight to join Old Croton Road (Route 129 west).
11.2	Right onto Hunterbrook Road.
13.1	Left onto Baptist Church Road.
13.9	Left onto Croton Avenue.
15.5	Right onto Yorktown Road (Route 129 west).
17.1	Left into Croton Gorge Park. When exiting the park, turn right and continue back the way you came.
18.0	Right onto Croton Dam Road.
18.9	Right onto Yorktown Road.
19.3	Left onto Apple Bee Farm Road (later changes names to Blinn Road).
20.5	Right onto Spring Valley Road.
20.9	Right into Teatown Lake Reservation. When exiting, return to the Spring Valley-Blinn intersection.
21.3	Right to continue on Spring Valley Road.
21.9	Left onto Kitchewan Road (Route 134 east).
24.4	Left onto Somerstown Turnpike (Route 100 north).
25.9	Left over bridge across reservoir.
26.2	Continue straight on Route 100 north.
30.7	Right at intersection with Route 35.
32.6	Back into Katonah.

frequently changing exhibits. Another spot worth a visit is the Katonah Deli across the road—a great place to fuel up for the ride ahead!

On this trip you will tour the reservoir that almost sunk the town. **Croton Reservoir** is a scenic body of water that provides a great backdrop for cycling. Begin at the corner of Jay Street (known officially as the Parkway at this point) and Bedford Road, heading north out of town on the latter. Bear left at the end of Bedford onto Route 35. In about a mile you will catch your first view of the water.

Entering the town of Somers, watch for the sign proclaiming this as the BIRTHPLACE OF THE AMERICAN CIRCUS (more about this later). At the junction with Somerstown Turnpike (Route 100), turn left and begin the journey along the reservoir's north shore. This road is one of the county's best for cycling thanks to its wide shoulder—and the view isn't bad either!

One mile later keep an eye out for a sign on the right leading into **Muscoot Farm**. The farm was owned by the Hopkins family for three generations. It was sold to Westchester County in 1968 and subsequently enlarged to its present 777 acres. Not just a museum to the past, the farm is a true working agricultural complex. During any given visit you might find cows being milked, sheep being shorn, or fields being sown, weeded, or harvested. The main house was built in the 1880s and relocated to its present site in 1894, the year of the flood. It is currently used for cooking demonstrations, classes, and art exhibits. Trails extend throughout the farm; the longest (the "yellow" trail) can be hiked in about two hours.

Route 100 crosses Croton Reservoir on its way toward Millwood, but the ride continues to the right on Lake Road (Route 118). After 1 mile Route 118 takes a right, but you should continue straight on Old Croton Road (Route 129). You will immediately notice two things about Routes 118 and 129: they are both much narrower and much hillier than Route 100! But the striking scenery will make the aches worth it.

Just before Route 129 crosses over the reservoir on Hunter Bridge, turn right onto Hunterbrook Road. Once again the hills come on strong as the road winds northward along a small inlet off the reservoir. In about 2 miles a quick left turn at a four-way intersection brings you onto Baptist Church Road. Another left onto Croton Avenue takes you southward along the opposite bank of Hunters Brook Cove. At the road's end rejoin Route 129 and continue westward. [If your legs are not up to the hills of Hunterbrook Road, continue straight across the bridge instead.]

After passing the left turn onto Croton Dam Road, take the next left off Route 129 into **Croton Gorge Park**. (The entrance is midway down a steep hill.) The park, surrounding the base of Croton Dam, offers an unparalleled view of the reservoir's overflow waters crashing through the dam's gates and over man-made waterfalls. Footpaths take hikers through the park, while a shaded picnic area makes a pleasant midride resting spot.

Back on the bike, return to Route 129 and turn right on Croton Dam Road (whew, what a hill!), crossing the dam itself. Continue to the road's end; then bear right for a short stint on Yorktown Road. At the next left, turn onto Apple Bee Farm Road and begin another climb. You will pass the farm itself toward the hill's peak. A little farther along the road changes names to Blinn Road. Regardless of the label, the trip is curvy and bumpy and must be ridden cautiously.

Blinn soon ends at Spring Valley Road. Turning right on Spring Valley, you will come to **Teatown Lake Reservation** over the first hill. The reservation began development in 1963 after the county was given 190 acres by the Gerard Swope family. Centrally located in the reservation is a beautiful 33-acre lake surrounded by marshland, forest, and meadows. Hiking trails lead away from the visitors' center and pass throughout the property. One path, called the "Back 40" trail, offers a spectacular 10-mile view of the lower Hudson Valley. Many visitors come to enjoy the colorful wildflowers or the many songbirds that call Teatown home, while others simply come to enjoy the silence and serenity.

Return to the Spring Valley-Blinn intersection for the half-mile trek to Kitchewan Road (Route 134). From Kitchewan take a left onto Somerstown Turnpike (Route 100 north) and proceed across Croton Reservoir for the trip home.

If you have a little extra energy, rather than heading immediately back to Katonah, why not continue north into the center of Somers (about 4 miles farther up Route 100). As the sign proclaimed earlier, Somers is the birthplace of the American circus. The story begins in 1825 when Hachaliah Bailey built a hotel in the center of town. He named the building the **Elephant Hotel** to commemorate Old Bet, an African elephant he had purchased ten years earlier. Bailey created a "rolling menagerie" of animals that traveled across the countryside. Thus, the traveling circus was born.

Today the Elephant Hotel acts as the Somers Town Hall as well as the home of the Somers Historical Society. Inside, a small museum tracing the history of the circus is open on Friday afternoons and Saturday mornings. Admission is free. Across the street a small statue immortalizes Old Bet for all to see.

For Further Information

Katonah Gallery (914) 232–4988
Muscoot Farm (914) 232–7118
Croton Gorge Park (914) 271–3293
Teatown Lake Reservation (914) 762–2912
Elephant Hotel (914) 277–4977

Getting There

By car, take Exit 6 off Interstate 684 and follow the signs to the Katonah railroad station. For railroaders, take Metro North from Grand Central Station to the Katonah train station.

Westchester County
Titicus Reservoir Quickie

Mileage:	12 (24 with optional side trip)
Approximate pedaling time:	2 hours
Terrain:	Rolling
Traffic:	Mostly light
Things to see:	Titicus Reservoir, North Salem Historic District, Hammond Museum, Balanced Rock, Ward Pound Ridge Reservation (optional), Mill's Road Cemetery

Cycling the roads of upper Westchester can be both an exhausting and an exhilarating experience. Many long, high hills test a cyclist's conditioning and endurance. Here is a short ride that offers a little relief from all that, while still including a few challenging climbs.

Begin in Purdys at the intersection of Routes 22 and 116, which is directly accessible from Exit 7 off Interstate 684. There is ample parking along the roadside for those who must drive to the departure point, as well as a deli in case you want to stock up on provisions before leaving.

Head north on Routes 22/116, turning to the right just ahead as Route 116 (Titicus Road) veers to the east. **Titicus Reservoir** will soon appear through the trees on the right. The reservoir supplies water to New York City, while its shoreline supplies cyclists with a wonderful natural setting.

At the reservoir's east end continue on Route 116 as Turkey Hill Road intersects from the right. You will soon pass Salem Center, the site of the North Salem Town Hall in the town's **historic district.** Next door is the Delancy House (built in 1770) and a monument honoring the fallen soldiers of World War I.

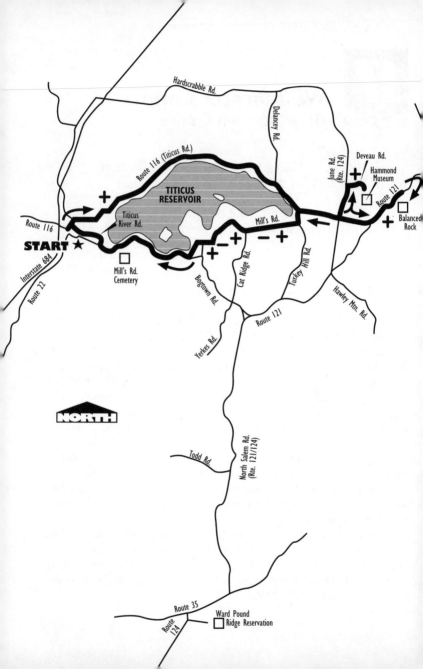

DIREC-TIONS at a glance

0.0	Start at the intersection of Interstate 684, Route 22, and Route 116.
0.1	Right on Route 116 east toward North Salem.
3.4	Left at triangle.
3.9	Left at stop sign onto Route 124.
4.3	Right onto Deveau Road.
4.9	At road's end, turn left to Hammond Museum. Afterward, head back down Deveau Road.
5.5	Left on Route 124.
5.9	Right on Route 116.
6.5	Left onto Routes 116/121.
7.0	Balanced Rock on right. Afterward, turn around.
7.5	Turn right on Route 116 West.
8.6	Left onto Turkey Hill Road.
8.7	Right on Mill's Road
10.5	Right at stop sign to stay on Mill's Road.
11.0	Right onto Titicus River Road.
12.2	Left on Route 22 to the beginning of the ride.

Turn left at the four-way intersection with Route 124 (June Road). Just up the road on the left is the June Cemetery. Within its walls are headstones that date back to 1806.

After you pass the cemetery get ready to turn right on Deveau Road. Although it extends for only 0.6 mile, Deveau is the most challenging part of the ride thanks to a steep profile and rugged surface. You might find it easier just to walk its length. Deveau, a dead-end street, stops at the entrance to the **Hammond Museum.** The museum, open Wednesday through Sunday afternoons, features beautifully landscaped gardens and elegantly furnished rooms. There is a small charge for admission.

Head back down Deveau (careful—remember the bumps) to Route 124. Turn left and backtrack to the intersection with Route 116; take another left. Just beyond the intersection is the Saint James Episcopal Church, in use since 1750.

Follow Route 116 left (east) as it joins Route 121 toward North Salem. In about 0.5 mile you will come to a most curious sight: **Balanced Rock.** According to a nearby sign, the rock—which is actually a ninety-ton boulder perched atop five smaller rocks—is a relic of the most recent ice age. Not everyone agrees with this theory, however. A different school of thought calls it a *dolmen* or *stone table.* In his book *America, B.C.* (Quadrangle Press, 1976), Barry Fell likens Balanced Rock to many similar rock formations found in New England as well as northern Europe that are thought to have been created by ancient civilizations such as the Celts or the Iberians long before the birth of Christ. Balanced Rock is the largest example of a dolmen yet found in North America. While Fell's evidence is not totally compelling, it makes interesting food for thought.

Backtrack again to the intersection of Routes 116 and 121. If you wish to double the ride's length, continue straight on Route 121 South. In about 6 miles Route 121 will have wound its way toward the entrance of the **Ward Pound Ridge Reservation.** This 4,700-acre park boasts facilities for hiking, swimming, and picnicking. It is a wonderful place to spend the day or an entire weekend! Open-faced lean-tos are available for camping year-round (tents are not permitted). If you have always yearned to try bicycle camping but don't want to travel too far from home, Pound Ridge Reservation is the place to go. Afterward, return along Route 121 North to the intersection with Route 116.

To continue back toward Purdys, follow Route 116 to the west. After passing the North Salem Town Hall (this time on the right), turn left onto Turkey Hill Road and then right onto Mill's Road. Both begin with lovely open farmland. As Mill's Road continues to roll across hill and dale, the pastoral expanses give way to the wooded south shore of Titicus Reservoir.

About 0.3 mile after the right-hand turn at the Bogtown Road intersection, watch for the **Mill's Road Cemetery** on the left. Dating back to 1784, this small cemetery is immaculately maintained by the North Salem Historical Society.

Not far beyond the cemetery turn right onto Titicus River Road. After a quick drop-off, the road takes you back to Routes 22 and 116.

For Further Information

Hammond Museum (914) 669–5135
Ward Pound Ridge Reservation (914) 763–3993

Getting There

The ride's starting point is directly adjacent to Exit 7 off Interstate 684. Metro North provides railroad service from New York's Grand Central Station to Purdys, directly adjacent to the ride's starting point.

Putnam County
Brewster to Carmel

Mileage:	30
Approximate pedaling time:	5 hours
Terrain:	Hilly
Traffic:	Moderate in the village centers, light elsewhere
Things to see:	Middle Branch Reservoir, Croton Falls Reservoir, Croton Dam, Carmel Historical District, Lake Mahopac, West Branch Reservoir, Lake Gleneida Park

Like Westchester County to its south, much of Putnam County is wet with reservoirs. On this ride you will circle some of the county's larger bodies of water and witness some spectacular scenery along the way.

Beginning at the Brewster railroad station, head north on U.S. Route 6. In just under a mile, turn left onto Drewville Road (shown as County Route 36 on some maps). You will soon catch your first glimpse of **Middle Branch Reservoir** on the right. Continuing along Drewville, cross a short and then a long breakwater over a second reservoir, **Croton Falls Reservoir.**

When you come to a four-way intersection, turn left onto Stoneleigh Avenue (County Route 35). Highlighted by the Putnam Community Hospital about 0.5 mile later on the left, Stoneleigh is mostly wooded and undeveloped. About 0.7 mile after crossing a third breakwater over Croton Falls Reservoir, turn right onto unmarked Croton Dam Road (this intersection is *very* easy to ride right by; if you come to a major intersection with Route 22, you have gone about 0.5 mile too far.)

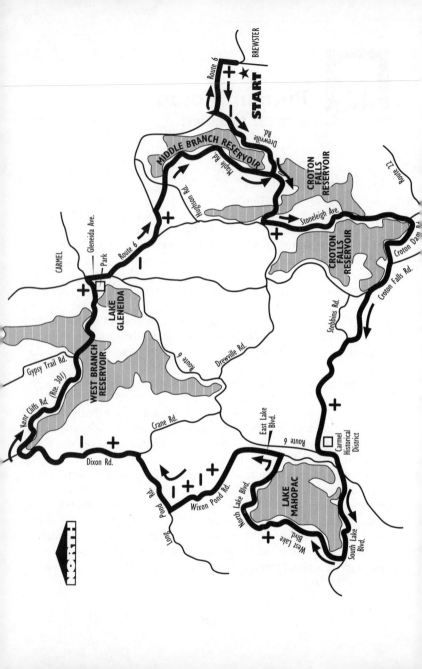

NORTH

START

BREWSTER

Route 6

Drewville Rd.

MIDDLE BRANCH RESERVOIR

Maple Rd.

Highbon Rd.

CROTON FALLS RESERVOIR

Route 22

Stoneleigh Ave.

CROTON FALLS RESERVOIR

Croton Dam Rd.

Gleneida Ave.

Route 6

Park

CARMEL

LAKE GLENEIDA

Croton Falls Rd.

Gypsy Trail Rd.

WEST BRANCH RESERVOIR

Kent Cliffs Rd. (Rte. 301)

Route 6

Drewville Rd.

Stebbins Rd.

Crane Rd.

East Lake Blvd.

Carmel Historical District

Route 6

Dixon Rd.

Long Pond Rd.

Wixon Pond Rd.

North Lake Blvd.

LAKE MAHOPAC

West Lake Blvd.

South Lake Blvd.

0.0   Leave the Brewster railroad station, heading
       north on Route 6.
0.9   Left onto Drewville Road.
3.2   Left onto Stoneleigh Avenue.
5.2   Right on Croton Dam Road (unmarked).
6.4   Merge right onto Croton Falls Road.
9.8   Left onto Route 6.
10.7 Right onto South Lake Boulevard (Route 6N).
12.0 Right onto West Lake Boulevard. Road will change names
       to North Lake Boulevard.
14.8 Left onto East Lake Boulevard (Msgr. O'Brien Cooney Road).
15.3 Left onto Wixon Pond Road.
17.1 Right onto Long Pond Road.
18.1 Left onto Dixon Road at Mahopac Volunteer Fire Department.
20.1 Right onto Kent Cliffs Road (Route 301).
23.0 Right onto Gleneida Avenue.
23.4 Left on Route 6 at stop light.
24.7 Right on Maple Road (unmarked).
25.0 Straight at four-way split.
27.2 Left on Drewville Road.
28.5 Right on Route 6.
29.5 Finish at the Brewster railroad station.

Croton Dam Road is the first of two dirt roads encountered on the ride. (It is also the better maintained of the two and should be passable, with caution, on all bikes.) About 0.25 mile in, the road swings across the **dam** itself, offering an unparalleled view of the reservoir and its shoreline. After passing the dam stay to the right at the fork and continue to the road's end. [If you want to stay on blacktop instead, continue straight on Stoneleigh Avenue all the way to its end at Route 22, where you will turn right. Route 22 soon forks to the left; stay to the right on Route 202. A little farther along, turn right again, this time onto Croton Falls Road (County Route 34) to pick up the ride.]

Merge to the right as Croton Dam Road intersects Croton Falls Road (County Route 34), which will lead you all the way into Mahopac. If time permits take a short side trip to the **Carmel Historical District**. Keep an eye out for a sign directing you to the left just before downtown Mahopac. There you may explore a bit of county and local history.

At the end of Croton Falls Road, turn left onto Route 6. Although the road is heavily traveled, you will be on it for only a short while. In about 0.5 mile veer right on South Lake Boulevard (Route 6N). The route continues to the right on West Lake Boulevard and then North Lake Boulevard, circling about three-quarters of **Lake Mahopac**. Unlike the reservoirs (access to which is closely regulated), Lake Mahopac is a recreational paradise, offering boating, sailing, swimming, and fishing. You might want to pause at the Mahopac Snack Bar on South Lake Boulevard for a lakeside lunch.

After you pass the Mahopac Golf Club at the end of North Lake Boulevard, turn left onto East Lake Boulevard (also known as Msgr. O'Brien Cooney Road); take another left onto Wixon Pond Road. (Look for the pond itself about 0.5 mile later on the left.) The latter road is characterized by lots of short-but-steep ups and downs, resulting in a roller-coaster-like ride.

Next, bear right onto Long Pond Road (County Route 32). You'll see Long Pond through the trees on the right. About a mile later turn left at the Mahopac Volunteer Fire Department onto Dixon Road. Dixon is also a bit of a roller coaster, ending at the northern tip of the **West Branch Reservoir**.

Continue to the right onto Kent Cliffs Road (Route 301), following the reservoir's eastern shore. You will welcome the smooth riding surface! After 3 miles you will have wound your way into the village of Carmel. Straight ahead is the Putnam County Courthouse (dated 1814), while on the right is a pleasant town park along **Lake Gleneida**. The park makes a wonderful place to stop and rest a while and is also the site of a statue honoring Revolutionary War heroine Sybil Ludington.

Follow the signs for Route 6 east as you exit Carmel. About 1.3 miles later, just as the shoulder of Route 6 degenerates to not much more than a rock-strewn footpath, turn right at a four-way intersection onto Maple Road. Maple is unmarked, but you will see it coming at the top of a hill. The road soon splits into three—choose the middle lane. Although the road changes to a hard-packed dirt surface for about 1 mile of its 2.5-mile length, Maple offers outstanding scenery as it winds along the western bank of Middle Branch Reservoir. (For a paved alternative, continue along Route 6 to the intersection with Drewville Road on the way back to Brewster.)

As Maple Road ends bear left onto Drewville Road. At the end of Drewville turn right on Route 6 for the 1-mile sprint back to the Brewster railroad station.

For Further Information

Putnam County Historical Society (914) 265–4010

Getting There

Brewster is located at the intersection of Route 22 and Interstates 84 and 684, making it easily accessible from the entire tristate region. For those who prefer to use mass transit, take Metro North's Harlem line to the Brewster railroad station.

Rockland County
Hudson River Loop

Mileage:	26
Approximate pedaling time:	4 hours
Terrain:	Rolling to extremely hilly
Traffic:	Light to moderate
Things to see:	Hudson River, Rockland Lake State Park, Tappan Zee Bridge, Onderdonk House, Blauvelt Interstate Park, Johannes Blauvelt Homestead, Clarksville Inn, Lake De Forest

The **Hudson River** is considered one of the most beautiful rivers in the country, if not the world. Touring its banks by bicycle offers some outstanding scenery and some spectacular challenges.

Begin from parking field #1 at **Rockland Lake State Park**, one of a chain of parks that comprise the Palisades Interstate Park System. Exiting through the park's south exit, continue straight across Route 9W onto Rockland Lake Road. Though it climbs at first, Rockland Lake Road is mostly flat. At its end turn sharply to the left on Cristian Herald Road. Cristian Herald presents the first real challenge of the ride as it is up, up, and away for nearly 0.75 mile.

At the end of Cristian Herald Road continue straight across Route 9W onto Old Mountain Road. Try not to build up too much speed going down the old mountain because at its bottom, around a sharp right turn, Old Mountain Road shoots off to the left. If you are going too fast, you will miss the intersection (we have!) and end up on Midland Avenue.

Old Mountain Road ends at a T intersection with Broadway. Turning right, our route now travels southward along the Hudson's west bank. In between the road and the river are many stately homes.

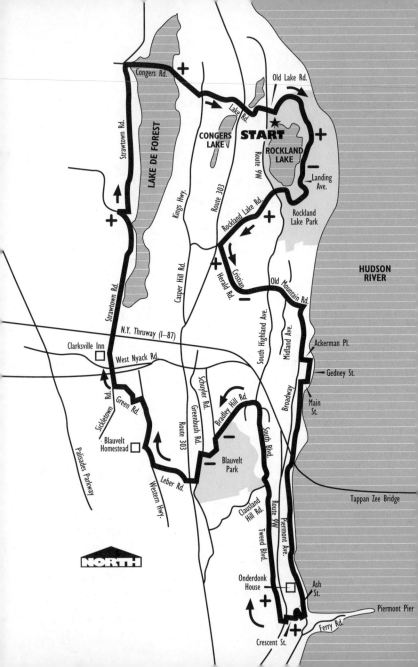

0.0	Right out of parking field #1 in Rockland Lake State Park.
1.0	Right at T onto Landing Road.
2.5	Leave park at south exit and cross Route 9W onto Rockland Lake Road.
3.7	Left onto Cristian Herald Road.
4.8	Cross Route 9W onto Old Mountain Road.
5.6	Right onto Broadway.
6.4	Left onto Ackerman Place.
6.5	Right onto Gedney Street.
6.7	Right onto Main Street.
6.8	Left onto Piermont Avenue.
10.2	Right onto Ash Street.
10.6	Right onto Crescent Street.
10.7	Left onto Route 9W.
10.8	Right onto Tweed Blvd.
13.1	Right onto Clausland Hill Road (South Boulevard). Go straight for "gravelly" shortcut through Blauvelt Park.
14.0	Left onto South Highland Avenue.
14.2	Right onto Bradley Hill Road (unmarked).
15.6	Left onto Greenbush Road.
15.9	Cross Route 303 onto Leber Road.
16.0	At T continue to the right on Leber.
16.7	Right onto Western Highway.
17.7	Left onto Green Road.
18.4	Right onto County Route 23 (Sickletown Road/ Strawtown Road).
23.2	Right onto Congers Road (County Route 80).
24.5	Follow County Route 80 (now called Lake Road) through Congers.
25.5	Follow County Route 80 to the left onto Old Lake Road.
25.6	Cross Route 9W to Rockland Lake State Park.

There is also a nice deli down the road on the right if you want to stop for a quick refueling or to pick up lunch. Broadway is marked with many green-and-white BIKE ROUTE signs, which will help you navigate through the center of Nyack in the miles to come.

Following the posted bike route, turn left onto Ackerman Place and take a fast plunge down toward the river. Then take two quick rights and a left to wind up on Piermont Avenue. Piermont is a long, flat stretch that runs right along the Hudson.

About a mile later pass under the **Tappan Zee Bridge** and enter the village of Grand-View-On-Hudson. Many Victorian homes line the street, reflecting the glory of a bygone era.

As you approach the center of Piermont, keep an eye out for Ritie Street. On the corner is a bronze plaque marking the **Onderdonk House**. This was the 1783 site where George Washington met with leaders of the British army and where Britain first officially recognized the United States as an independent nation.

As you enter Piermont you have the option of continuing straight to Tallman Mountain State Park or turning left to the Piermont Pier. Our route, however, bears right and heads up Ash Street. And we do mean up! Ash is an incredible climb that is best walked.

Follow Ash to Crescent Street; turn right. Crescent ends shortly at Route 9W. Turn left, followed by a quick right onto Tweed Boulevard—drat, uphill again! Happily, you can put away the mountain-climbing gear as the hill crests; Tweed is mostly flat from here on. Take our word for it, the views of the Hudson will have made the climb worth it.

Tweed Boulevard ends at a four-way intersection with Clausland Hill Road. It is now decision time. Straight ahead is the road into **Blauvelt Interstate Park.** Unfortunately, the park road shortly changes to gravel, making bicycling impractical. Still, if you have an ATB, it might be an exciting diversion. If you choose the park route, proceed all the way through to Bradley Hill Road.

If you choose the smoother route, take a right onto Clausland, which later changes to South Boulevard. Turn left onto South Highland Avenue and then right onto unmarked Bradley Hill Road. Bradley Hill offers abundant shade, and for once the road is going in the right direction—downhill.

Continue until you reach a four-way intersection with Greenbush Road; turn left. Cross Route 303 onto Leber Road. Follow Leber to the right after crossing a rather rickety railroad bridge and continue all the way to the road's end at Western Highway, where you will turn right. About 0.5 mile after joining Western Highway, watch for a historical marker in front of a Dutch farmhouse on the left. This is the **Johannes Blauvelt Homestead**, site of the first U.S. tobacco company.

The route next turns left onto Green Road and then right onto Sickletown Road (County Route 23). Just ahead on the left is a marker pointing to **Clarksville Inn**, an early stagecoach stop. Continuing north on County Route 23 (now called Strawtown Road), watch for the first signs of **Lake De Forest** to the east just before the road makes a sharp right-hand turn. You will get a much better view of this beautiful body of water as you approach the intersection with Congers Road (County Route 80).

Follow County Route 80 east all the way into Congers. Although the road changes names to Lake Road and later Old Lake Road, stay on it through town. Popping out the other side of the town, you will come to Route 9W and the north entrance of Rockland Lake State Park. Welcome back.

For Further Information

Rockland Lake State Park (914) 268–3020 or (914) 268–7598
Clarksville Inn (914) 358–8899

Getting There

Rockland Lake State Park is located on Route 9W in Congers, about 3 miles north of Exit 11 on the New York State Thruway (Interstate 87).

Rockland County
Stony Point

Mileage:	9
Approximate pedaling time:	1.5 hours
Terrain:	Hilly
Traffic:	Moderate
Things to see:	Buckberg Mountain, Springsteel Farm marker, Bear Mountain State Park (optional), Stony Point State Park

Lying south of Bear Mountain State Park, the village of Stony Point is a serene hamlet blessed with a commanding view of the Hudson River. In colonial days Stony Point served as the western landing for a cross-river ferry that shuttled traffic over to Verplanck's Point on the eastern shore. The ferry was a vital link connecting New England with New Jersey, Pennsylvania, and the southern colonies.

In an effort to sever this all-important trade route during the Revolutionary War, British troops seized Stony Point on May 30, 1779. By this capture, Sir Henry Clinton, commander of the British force, had also successfully cut off General George Washington and the Continental Army from New York City.

Washington, realizing the importance of Stony Point, called in General Anthony Wayne to mastermind a plan to rid the town of the British Army. "Mad Anthony," so nicknamed for the apparent recklessness of the Stony Point campaign, was given full charge of more than 1,500 light infantrymen for the battle. You are about to trace much of the route used by Wayne and his troops as they fought to recapture Stony Point.

Depart from the Stony Ridge Plaza, located on Route 9W about a mile north of town. Head north on Route 9W. In 0.5 mile you will

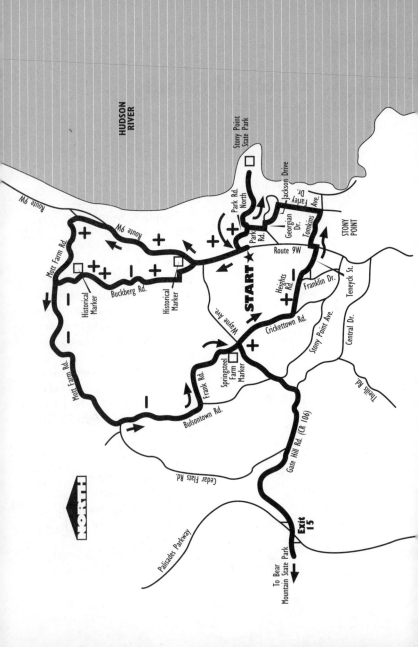

DIREC-TIONS at a glance

0.0	Head north on Route 9W out of Stony Ridge Shopping Plaza, about a mile north of the center of Stony Point.
0.5	Left onto Buckberg Road (optional—see text).
1.3	Left onto Mott Farm Road.
3.7	Left onto unmarked Bulsontown Road.
4.5	Left onto Frank Road.
5.4	Straight onto Crickettown Road.
5.9	Left onto Heights Road.
6.4	Left onto Ten Eyck Street.
6.6	Left onto Route 9W; then right onto Tomkins Avenue.
6.9	Left onto Farley Drive.
7.2	Left onto Jackson Drive.
7.5	Left onto Georgian Drive.
7.6	Right onto Park Road. Continue into state park.
8.8	Exit park on Park Road North. Continue to end at Route 9W, then turn left.
9.1	Back at Stony Ridge Plaza.

pass Buckberg Road on the left. A small marker on the corner informs passersby that this was once an important military route that ran all the way to West Point. If you like mountain climbing you can continue on this road as it heads up and over **Buckberg Mountain.**

A second historical marker farther up Buckberg Road on the right indicates the site where Washington and Wayne surveyed the British encampment at Stony Point while plotting a strategy for the attack. None of the trees and brush that block the river view today existed two centuries ago (they were all brought in earlier this century by homeowners and developers). From atop this rocky knoll the generals had a clear view of the enemy's actions.

If you want to avoid the climb over Buckberg Mountain, stay on northbound Route 9W into Tomkins Cove and turn left onto Mott Farm Road (County Route 118). Although Mott Farm begins with an uphill climb, it is still the lesser of two evils. Besides, in only a mile or so it begins a long, pleasant downhill run. Up ahead, at a ⊤ intersection, turn left onto unmarked Bulsontown Road and continue downhill.

The hill continues beyond the left turn you must take onto Frank Road, so be sure not to zip right by. Be on the lookout for overhead high-voltage wires; you pass under them just before the turn. Frank Road (sometimes spelled *Franck*) dates to pre-Revolutionary times, when it extended over the Ramapo Mountains. It was along Frank Road, at the **Springsteel Farm**, that Wayne and his squad assembled before they broke for the attack on Stony Point. Though the farm is long gone, a handmade **marker** hidden in the woods on the right across from Boy Scout Camp Bulowa marks the site of the farmhouse.

Wayne split his troops into three large divisions. One was to attack from the north, one from the south, and the third directly from the west. The troops left the farm just before midnight, traveling southward on Frank Road. At the next intersection (now known as Wayne Road), the northern division split off to the left, while the others continued on Crickettown Road, just as you will.

Before proceeding down Crickettown, you may wish to extend the ride into nearby **Bear Mountain State Park**. If so, follow Wayne Road to the right all the way to its end at Gate Hill Road (County Route 106). Turn right onto Gate Hill and continue into the park. Mile after mile of pleasant (albeit hilly) cycling await anyone who roams into the park. For more information on the park's roads, trails, and other features, call the park information office at the telephone number listed at the end of this ride.

Back on track with General Wayne, continue on Crickettown Road to Heights Road, where the route bears left just before a steep downgrade. Follow a zigzag path through town on Ten Eyck Street to Route 9W and finally onto Tomkins Avenue. Though Wayne's men assaulted the point by moving right along the river's edge, the bike route follows a somewhat drier approach. Bear left onto Farley Drive and weave your way onto Jackson, then Georgian, followed by a right onto Park Road. Take this all the way to **Stony Point State Park**.

Upon entering the park dismount your bike next to the museum entrance and step inside to finish the story of the battle. As the exhibits explain, Wayne and his troops successfully recaptured Stony Point from the British in less than an hour, though not without cost. Fifteen Americans were killed and eighty-three wounded, while the British suffered twenty casualties and seventy-four wounded. Many mementos on display in the museum remain as a testimony to the bravery of the soldiers who fought to secure our young country's freedom. Maps are available that guide visitors along the park's footpaths past many of the battle's key sites. Of special interest is the location of the Britishers' main redoubt perched atop a rock outcropping at the highest tip of the point. The park is open Wednesdays through Sundays from 8:30 A.M. to 5:00 P.M.

Return from the park as you entered along Park Road. Turn right onto Park Road North and continue to its end at Route 9W. Bear left and return to the shopping center from which you began. Congratulations—you, too, have conquered Stony Point.

For Further Information

Stony Point State Park (914) 786–2521
Bear Mountain State Park (914) 786–2701

Getting There

Stony Point lies south of Bear Mountain State Park and the Bear Mountain Bridge. From New York City the most direct approach is from the Palisades Interstate Parkway. Take Exit 15 (Gate Hill Road—County Route 106) and head east. Turn left onto Route 9W and proceed through the center of town to Stony Ridge Plaza.

Orange County
Monroe to Chester

Mileage:	16
Approximate pedaling time:	2 hours
Terrain:	Moderately hilly
Traffic:	Light
Things to see:	Round Lake, Walton Lake, Sugar Loaf village, Museum Village

In many ways, residents of Orange County have the best of both worlds. On one hand, they bask in beautiful rural surroundings of farms, pastures, and small towns. On the other, they enjoy easy access to New York City, which lies a scant 40 miles down the Hudson River. You are about to tour some of the county's loveliest lakes, farms, and meadows. Along the way you can choose to visit two villages that are unlike any others in the tristate region.

From the center of Monroe pedal south on Lake Road (County Route 5). About 0.25 mile along on the left, watch for a small pond fed by a charming little waterfall. A waterwheel stands ready for action, but its weathered face seems to say that it has lain dormant for years.

Even though its shoulders are narrow, Lake Road is great for bicycling. And it certainly is appropriately named, as you are about to discover. Just over the next hill, **Round Lake**, one of two large bodies of water along this road, greets you on the right. The small park along the shore of Round Lake is a perfect place to pull over for a roadside picnic.

Continue down Lake Road along the water's edge; be careful, as the road is narrow in spots. A second hill lies between Round Lake and **Walton Lake**. Once ascended, however, the peak provides a nice view of the lake and its beautiful environment.

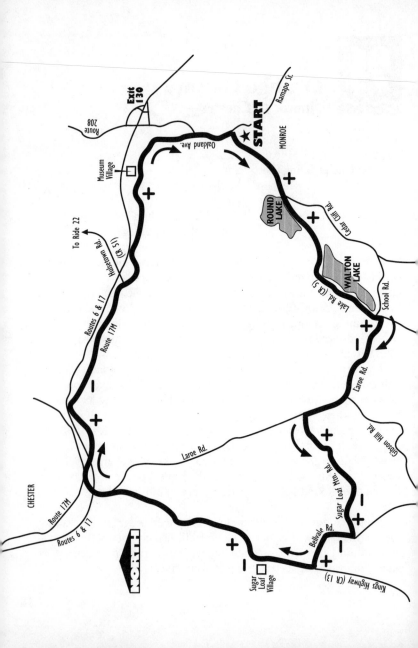

NORTH

Exit 130

Route 208

Museum Village

To Ride 22

Halsetown Rd. (CR 51)

Routes 6 & 17

Route 17M

CHESTER

Routes 6 & 17

Route 17M

Laroe Rd.

Sugar Loaf Village

Sugar Loaf Mtn. Rd.

Bellvale Rd.

Kings Highway (CR 13)

Gibson Hill Rd.

Laroe Rd.

Lake Rd. (CR 5)

School Rd.

WALTON LAKE

ROUND LAKE

Cedar Cliff Rd.

Oakland Ave.

START

MONROE

Ramapo St.

DIREC-TIONS at a glance	0.0	Head south on Lake Road (County Route 5) from Route 17M away from the center of Monroe.
	3.1	Right onto Laroe Road.
	4.6	Left onto Sugar Loaf Mountain Road.
	6.3	Right onto Bellvale Road.

7.0   Right onto Kings Highway (County Route 13).
10.3 Right onto Route 17M heading east.
15.7 Back at the corner of Lake Road and Route 17M.

Just past the southern tip of Walton Lake, turn right onto Laroe Road. Though it begins with a mild uphill notch, Laroe quickly changes profile to a long, downhill run that lasts for nearly 1.5 miles. Close to the bottom turn left onto Sugar Loaf Mountain Road. While it is less than 2 miles long, this is the toughest stretch of road on the entire ride. The first half is especially challenging! If you are like us, though, the pain in your legs will be tempered by the scenic beauty of the area.

Sugar Loaf Mountain Road ends at unmarked Bellvale Road, where the ride turns right. The barns and silos seen in the distance clearly show that much of Orange County is still agricultural.

A right turn onto Kings Highway (County Route 13) takes you into the magical village of **Sugar Loaf**. This wonderful town has more than fifty small shops where talented artisans display and sell their handmade crafts. Stores of all sorts line Kings Highway, with many dating back to the town's origin in 1749. Among our favorites is Grandma Pat's Doll Museum. Three thousand dolls from around the world and across various time periods line grandma's walls. Nearby, the Exposures Gallery features original photographic art that is truly one-of-a-kind. Another unique shop is Basic Blue, with a marvelous collection of kaleidoscopes, chess sets, and cards. If all this has made you hungry, stop by one of the many food emporiums in town. They range from formal restaurants to a pizzeria, a deli, and Joan's Cones (an ice cream parlor). Need we say more?

Several special events are held at Sugar Loaf annually. Among these are the Spring Festival on Memorial Day weekend, an antique car show in August, and the Fall Festival in October. Concerts are held during the warmer months; call ahead for the schedule.

Beyond Sugar Loaf the road slides down a small hill, crosses the railroad tracks, then ascends past many acres of open farmland. Kings Highway soon flattens out for the 2-mile trek toward Chester. At Route 17M the ride continues to the right, but if you need to touch civilization (for food, restrooms, etc.), turn left to enter the town itself.

As you head east on Route 17M, the pastoral surroundings continue on the right side of the road; on your left are heavily traveled Routes 6 and 17. The contrast is striking! After climbing a rather long hill, prepare yourself for the longest downhill run of the ride. This is just what the doctor ordered for a hot summer's day! [If it's a nice day, why not extend the ride into nearby Goshen and Washingtonville? Turn right near the bottom of the hill onto Hulsetown Road—County Route 51—for the 5-mile trip to pick up Ride #22.]

The slope of the road reverses itself as you approach **Museum Village** on the left. The village is an authentic re-creation of a colonial town dating to about 1800. Within, you can visit a blacksmith's shop, schoolhouse, general store, and more than twenty other exhibition buildings. Many feature live demonstrations by villagers dressed in authentic period garb. Museum Village is open Wednesdays through Sundays from May to December. There is a charge for admission.

From here it's just a short trip back into Monroe. If you wish, follow the green-and-white BIKE ROUTE sign across the road at the intersection with Route 208. It leads to a paved bike lane that is completely separated from the busy street. Farther along the path winds through a lovely town park encircling Mill Pond. Be watchful of the many pedestrians that also use the path. In just 0.5 mile you will be back at Lake Road, but you may prefer to continue touring the park on your own.

For Further Information

Sugar Loaf village (914) 469–4963
Museum Village (914) 782–8247

Getting There

Take the New York Thruway (Interstate 87) to Routes 6 and 17 (Exit 16). Proceed west to Exit 130, then south on Route 208 to Route 17M. Follow 17M into the center of Monroe.

22 Orange County
Goshen to Washingtonville

Mileage:	22
Approximate pedaling time:	3 hours
Terrain:	Rolling
Traffic:	Light
Things to see:	Historic Track, Trotting Horse Museum, Brotherhood Winery

Like the previous route, this ride takes cyclists through pastureland and woodland, touching a bit of American history along the way. We begin at the intersection of Church Street and Main Street (Route 207) in Goshen. Founded in 1714, the town has been the county seat since 1727. The pride that Goshen takes in its rich heritage is immediately apparent as you look around its central green. West of the green is the imposing façade of the Goshen United Methodist Church, while to its south is the majestic First Presbyterian Church of Goshen.

Several monuments around the green commemorate events and citizens important to local history. One of the more unusual is a special streetlight found at the corner of Church and Main. At the base of the lamp four sculpted black horses' heads commemorate the town's involvement with horse breeding and racing. Indeed, Goshen has been nicknamed the "cradle of the trotter."

North of the green, past the intersection with Park Place (on the right), stands one of the world's oldest harness-racing tracks. **Historic Track** has seen many racing firsts since it opened in the 1840s, including the first sub-two-minute mile by a trotter and the first half-mile track to join the Grand Circuit. More recently, the track became the sporting world's first national historic site.

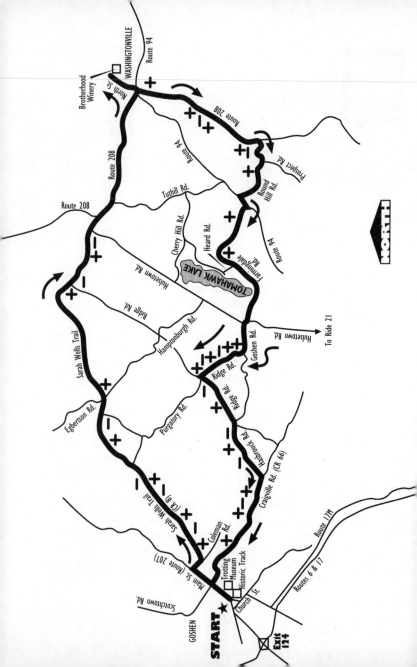

NORTH

Brotherhood Winery

WASHINGTONVILLE

North St.

Route 94

Route 208

Route 208

Route 208

Prospect Rd.

Round Hill Rd.

Route 94

Route 94

Tuthill Rd.

Cherry Hill Rd.

Heard Rd.

Farmingdale Rd.

TOMAHAWK LAKE

Hulsetown Rd.

Ridge Rd.

Hamptonburgh Rd.

Goshen Rd.

Hulsetown Rd.

To Ride 21

Sarah Wells Trail

Egbertson Rd.

Purgatory Rd.

Ridge Rd.

Ridge Rd.

Hasbrouck Rd.

Sarah Wells Trail (CR 8)

Coleman Rd.

Craigville Rd. (CR 66)

Main St. (Route 207)

Scotchtown Rd.

GOSHEN

START

Trotting Museum

Historic Track

Church St.

Route 17M

Routes 6 & 17

Exit 124

**DIREC-
TIONS
at a glance**

0.0	Begin at Goshen green at intersection with Main Street (Route 207) and Church Street.
1.0	Right onto Sarah Wells Trail (County Route 8).
1.1	Bear left to stay on Sarah Wells Trail.
7.6	Right onto Route 208.
9.7	Left onto Route 94 in center of Washingtonville.
9.8	Left onto North Street.
10.0	Right into Brotherhood Winery; turn around and return on North Street.
10.3	Right onto East Main Street (Route 94).
10.4	Left onto Route 208 (south).
12.7	Right onto Round Hill Road.
13.0	Right to stay on Round Hill Road.
13.8	Left onto Route 94.
13.9	Right onto Farmingdale Road.
16.1	Cross Hulsetown Road and continue on Goshen Road.
16.7	Right at stop sign onto unmarked Ridge Road (look for barn on right).
17.5	Left at stop sign to stay on Ridge Road.
18.4	Right at stop sign onto Hasbrouck Road.
19.4	Right onto Craigville Road (County Route 66).
21.3	Left at stop sign onto Main Street (Route 207).
21.8	Back at green.

Historic Track's rich past is well documented in the **Trotting Horse Museum** at 240 Main Street. Racing memorabilia, Currier and Ives prints, and more than 100 displays await visitors. The museum is open daily from 10 A.M. (noon on Sundays and holidays) until 5 P.M., and there is a small admission charge.

On the track side of Main Street, known as "Lawyers Row," are several beautifully maintained vintage homes. One of the more noteworthy is #210, a red-brick dwelling. There, in 1873, President Ulysses S. Grant stayed overnight to watch the races.

Leave Goshen on northbound Main Street and turn right onto Sarah Wells Trail (County Route 8) in about a mile. Miss Wells was the first European woman to settle in Goshen township in 1714. Her home was situated about 3 miles ahead on the right, though no trace of it exists nowadays.

While the trail begins in a typical suburban neighborhood, the homes are quickly replaced by cows and rolling pastures as you leave the town behind. There is one home, however, that is bound to attract your attention. To us it looks just like South Fork from the television series "Dallas!" You'll find it on the right at the top of a hill, about 3 miles after you turn onto the road (ironically, not far from where the humble Wells homestead once stood).

About a mile after you cross some railroad tracks, turn right onto Route 208. Follow this into Washingtonville, being especially careful of the bumps in the road as you approach the town's center. Take a left onto Route 94, followed almost immediately by another left onto North Street. **The Brotherhood Winery** awaits about 0.25 mile ahead on the right.

Brotherhood, which was founded in 1839, is America's oldest winery. If you have the time, why not join one of the guided tours available daily? They take just over an hour to complete. Special events are scheduled throughout the year, including harvest and grape-stomping festivals. Wine sampling is also available to tour groups, but remember, you're riding!

Return to southbound Route 208 (now called South Street) and head out of Washingtonville. Though the road begins on the bumpy side, it becomes smoother when it enters more rural environs, just over a small rise.

In a little more than 2 miles make a right onto Round Hill Road. Round Hill is characterized by rolling meadows peppered by a couple of short but steep climbs. At its end turn left onto Route 94, then right (just beyond an antique shop) onto Farmingdale Road. Farmingdale is thickly wooded, with few homes. Though the road is a bit secluded, the shade is welcome, especially on hot summer afternoons!

Not long after passing Heard Road on the right, keep an eye out on the same side for the southern tip of Tomahawk Lake. Tomahawk is a lovely body of water set in a beautiful valley. If you want an even better view of the lake, turn right onto Heard Road and continue to its end; then backtrack to Farmingdale.

At the end of Farmingdale Road cross Hulsetown Road (County Route 51) and continue straight on Goshen Road. [To extend the ride into nearby Chester and Monroe, follow Hulsetown to the left for 5 miles until it ends at Route 17M. There, pick up Ride #21.] Cross over the railroad tracks (careful, they are bumpy!) and begin a steep 0.5-mile climb. Turn right at the next stop sign onto unmarked Ridge Road and begin a roller-coaster trek over hill and dale.

Take a left at the stop sign to remain on Ridge Road, passing more open meadow along the way. Shortly, at a rather confusing four-way intersection, turn right onto Hasbrouck Road. Hasbrouck begins with an uphill sprint but finishes with a long descent.

For the ride's final leg turn right onto Craigville Road (County Route 66), followed by a left in 2 miles back onto Main Street (Route 207). From here it's only 0.5 mile to the center of Goshen.

For Further Information

Historic Track (914) 294–5333
Trotting Horse Museum (914) 294–6330
Brotherhood Winery (914) 496–9101

Getting There

Take the New York Thruway (Interstate 87) to Routes 6 and 17 (Exit 16). Head west to Exit 124 (Route 17A). Follow Route 17A into Goshen. Ample parking is available along Main Street.

Fairfield County
Greenwich

Mileage:	21
Approximate pedaling time:	3 hours
Terrain:	Hilly
Traffic:	Mostly light
Things to see:	Bruce Museum, Bruce Park, River-bridge Park, Rockwood Lake, Putnam Reservoir, Radio marker, Civil War monument

For many New Yorkers Greenwich, Connecticut, acts as the gateway to New England. But given that they live less than 40 miles from Times Square, most Greenwich residents probably align themselves more with the Big Apple than with, say, Boston. Greenwich offers an exquisite backdrop for many cycling adventures through the countryside. Here we offer just one possibility.

Depart from the intersection of Arch Street, Steamboat Road, Greenwich Avenue, and Museum Drive, proceeding eastward on the latter. Just up the hill on the left is a large mansion. The sign at its entrance tells you that this is the **Bruce Museum**. The museum features exhibits highlighting the arts and the sciences. Inside, displays of paintings, pottery, and costumes mingle with fossils and minerals. The museum also offers monthly lectures and films and hosts a number of local associations. It is open Tuesday through Sunday and asks for a small entrance donation.

Stay on Museum Drive all the way to its end at Indian Harbor Drive. There, a green-and-white sign declares this to be a designated bike route. Turn left onto Indian Harbor Drive, continuing straight at the next intersection to join Davis Avenue.

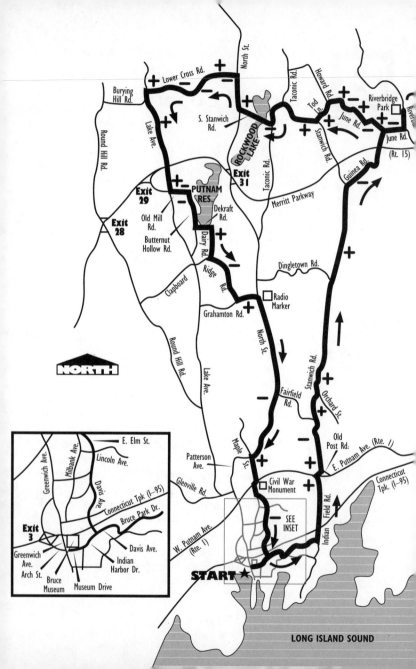

NORTH

LONG ISLAND SOUND

START ★

DIRECTIONS at a glance

0.0	Begin at the corner of Museum Drive and Greenwich Avenue.
0.2	Left onto Indian Harbor Drive.
0.3	Straight onto Davis Avenue.
0.6	Left onto Bruce Park Drive.
1.1	Left onto Indian Field Drive.

2.0	Cross East Putnam Avenue (Route 1); follow Old Post Road to right.
2.1	Left onto Stanwich Road.
3.2	Left to stay on Stanwich Road.
6.2	Right onto Guinea Road.
7.3	Right onto June Road.
7.5	Left onto Riverbank Road.
7.6	Left into Riverbridge Park.
7.7	Right onto June Road.
7.9	Right to stay on June Road.
9.0	Left onto Tod Lane.
9.3	Right onto Stanwich Road.
9.9	Straight onto Taconic Road.
10.3	Right onto South Stanwich Road.
10.8	Right onto North Street.
11.3	Left onto Lower Cross Road.
12.7	Left onto Lake Avenue.

14.1	Left onto Old Mill Road.
14.3	Right onto Butternut Hollow Road.
14.9	Left onto Dekraft Road.
15.2	Right onto Dairy Road.
15.5	Left onto Clapboard Ridge Road.
16.3	Left to stay on Clapboard Ridge Road.
16.6	Right onto North Street.
19.0	Left onto Maple Street.
19.3	Right onto East Putnam Avenue; then left onto Milbank Avenue.
19.6	Left onto East Elm Street.
19.9	Straight onto Davis Avenue.
20.1	Veer to the left to stay on Davis Avenue.
20.4	Right onto Indian Harbor Drive.
20.5	Right onto Museum Drive.
20.7	Back at starting point.

Just ahead cross a small bridge over Indian Harbor and turn left at the fork to enter **Bruce Park**, an especially beautiful public area. Ponds, walkways, playing fields, and tennis courts are found throughout for all to enjoy. A DUCK CROSSING sign warns all who pass to watch out for wandering waterfowl, which are especially prevalent in the spring when ducklings are hatched. You may wish to lean your bike against a tree and do a little wandering yourself along some of the park's paths. Our favorite leads from the road up a large rock out-cropping, where flowers blossom throughout the warmer months.

At the east end of Bruce Park Drive, veer left onto Indian Field Road. Be especially cautious after crossing over the Connecticut Turnpike (Interstate 95), as the road becomes rather narrow. Cross East Putnam Avenue (Route 1) onto Old Post Road, following the lat-ter as it hooks sharply to the right. Take the first left onto Stanwich Road for the (predominantly uphill) ride into northern Greenwich. Stanwich features lovely homes set on spacious estates. About a mile after joining Stanwich, a stop sign marks the intersection with Or-chard Street; the route follows Stanwich to the left. Even though Stan-wich has an uphill profile overall, its scenic, wooded surroundings and light traffic make it an idyllic thoroughfare for cyclists.

At the next stop sign, temporarily leave Stanwich Road to join Guinea Road on the right for a quick side trip into Stamford. A WIND-ING ROAD sign ahead warns you of things to come. Amid the curves the road pavement changes as you cross into Stamford. Guinea Road is mostly downhill and heavily wooded, making this a cool run even on hot summer days. Just be careful not to build up too much speed before negotiating a pair of sharp turns ahead.

Guinea Road ends abruptly at June Road, where the route takes a sharp right-hand turn. About 0.25 mile later, cross the Mianus River and turn left onto Riverbank Road. Follow Riverbank northward to the entrance into **Riverbridge Park** on the left. Though spartan, the park provides a lovely natural setting for a midride break. Walk your bike in a ways, secure it to a tree, and continue by foot toward a small man-made waterfall. On quiet mornings all you will hear are birds singing and the brook babbling.

Retreat back onto June Road, continuing past the Guinea Road turnoff. A hard, uphill mile later, leave June Road for Tod Lane on the left. Back in Greenwich, Tod lasts only a short distance and ends at Stanwich Road. Take a right up another hill, following Stanwich to its end at Taconic Road.

Continue straight after joining Taconic. Around the bend, take a right on South Stanwich Road. Coast down a pleasant drop toward **Rockwood Lake**, where you will have a great view of the water as you cycle over a small causeway. The scenery is magnificent all year but especially memorable in October when autumn's colors paint the landscape.

A right turn at the end of South Stanwich puts you on North Street, beginning with a difficult uphill sprint. It might be best to walk it unless you are in top condition. Thankfully, the road reverses its slope as it approaches the intersection with Lower Cross Road. Lower Cross has its ups and downs as it travels from one ridge to the next.

At the end of Lower Cross Road turn left onto Lake Avenue to begin the trip back toward the center of town. About 0.25 mile after crossing over the Merritt Parkway (Route 15), you will come to a stop sign. Take a left onto unmarked Old Mill Road; then a quick right onto Butternut Hollow Road. Butternut begins with a welcome downward slope, followed closely by a spectacular view of **Putnam Reservoir** through the trees on the left. You will cycle past the base of the dam forming the reservoir as you turn left onto Dekraft Road just beyond the lake's southern tip.

From Dekraft climb up Dairy Road, then coast down Clapboard Ridge Road back toward North Street. In the spring daffodils add color to the triangular island at the intersection of Clapboard Ridge and North. Adding even more color to the intersection is a **stone marker** proclaiming this to be a historic site. The monument re-counts that, near this spot on December 11, 1921, an amateur radio station sent the first transatlantic message on shortwave radio (to Ardrossan, Scotland).

Continue south on North. In the spring you'll pass countless daf-fodils and tulips in pastel colors of yellow, white, and red. Kind of makes you wonder where the yellow bricks are! At the end of North bear left onto Maple Street. Maple ends quickly at the intersection with East Putnam Avenue (Route 1). On the left corner stands a **monument** to the brave soldiers of the Civil War. A Union soldier stands atop a stone pillar that is carved with the names of some of the war's more important battles. On the same small plot of land a second marker commemorates the founding of Greenwich on July 18, 1640.

Zigzagging right and then left across Route 1, continue along Milbank Avenue. A series of quick left-hand turns will take you from Milbank to East Elm Street and ultimately to Davis Avenue. After passing under the railroad and Interstate 95, bear right on Davis for the trip back to Museum Drive and your starting point.

For Further Information

Bruce Museum (203) 869–0376

Getting There

The starting point is easily accessible from Exit 3 off Interstate 95. Head south on Arch Street and park along the road or in the huge parking lot directly adjacent to the railroad station. (Note parking restrictions.) For commuters, Greenwich's Metro-North train station is only a two-minute ride from the beginning of Museum Drive.

24 Fairfield County
Darien

Mileage:	14
Approximate pedaling time:	2 hours
Terrain:	Moderate to rolling
Traffic:	Potentially heavy around the center of town, light elsewhere
Things to see:	Darien Historical Society, Washington Marker, Pear Tree Point Beach, Webb House, Rings End Landing, Stephen Mather Homestead

Although the panhandle of southwestern Connecticut continues to develop as a series of bedroom communities for Manhattan executives, the towns have never lost their countrylike charm. Darien is but one such village that offers hours of pleasant cycling with minimal traffic hassles.

Begin your journey from the north exit of the Goodwives Shopping Center. There is ample parking here for those who must travel by car before departing. Bordering the shopping center to the north is the dark red colonial home of the **Darien Historical Society**. It houses a museum, which is open Thursday through Sunday afternoons. Admission is free. Both Goodwives Shopping Center and the Historical Society are located on Old Kings Highway, the first major thoroughfare to connect colonial New York City and Boston.

Exiting the shopping center, bear left and follow the route around to the Boston Post Road (Route 1). Proceed to the left on the Post Road through the center of town *carefully!* Passing under the Metro North railroad bridge, make a left onto Center Street at the second traffic light and wind your way to Locust Hill Road, heading toward Pear Tree Point. [If you are in the mood to ride a bit farther, turn left

NORTH

To
Ride
25

Talmadge Hill Rd.

Mather
Homestead

Stephen Mather Rd.

Ridge Rd.

Hollow Tree

Brookside Rd.

Hanson Rd.

Mansfield Ave. (Rt. 124)

Nutmeg Ln.

Darien
High School

High School Ln.

Hollow Tree Ridge Rd.

Middlesex Ave.

Stony Brook Rd.

Leroy Ave.

Old
Kings
Hwy.

Route 1

Connecticut Tpke. (I–95)

West Ave.

Sedgwick Ave.

Center St.

Darien Historical Society

Locust Hill Rd.

Noroton Ave.

Boston Post Rd.

Washington
Marker

Old
Kings
Hwy.

★ START
(Goodwives Ctr)

Rings End Rd.

Goodwives River Rd.

Webb House &
Rings End Landing

Pear Tree Pt. Rd.

Long Neck Pt. Rd.

Pear Tree
Point Beach

DIRECTIONS at a glance

0.0 Left out of the north exit of Goodwives Shopping Center onto Old Kings Highway.
0.1 Right at the island onto Sedgwick Avenue.
0.2 Left onto the Boston Post Road (Route 1).
0.4 Left onto Center Street.
0.5 Right onto Old Kings Highway.
0.7 Right onto Locust Hill Road.
1.2 Left onto Goodwives River Road.
2.2 Straight through stop sign and past fork.
3.3 Left onto Long Neck Point Road.
3.9 At intersection, continue to the right as Long Neck Point Road merges into Pear Tree Point Road. Just ahead, turn left onto Rings End Road.
4.5 Left onto the Boston Post Road (Route 1).
4.6 Right onto Noroton Avenue.
5.3 Right onto West Avenue.
6.1 Left onto Stony Brook Road.
6.4 Right to continue on Stony Brook Road.
6.8 At island, stay right to join Middlesex Avenue.
6.9 Left onto High School Lane.
7.1 Right through Darien High School campus, exiting through the parking lot onto Nutmeg Lane.
7.6 Right onto Hollow Tree Ridge Road.
7.8 Left to stay on Hollow Tree Ridge Road.
9.3 At stop sign, continue left around the curve.
10.2 Right onto Talmadge Hill Road.
10.6 Right onto Mansfield Avenue (Route 124).
10.7 Left onto Stephen Mather Road.
11.3 Right onto Brookside Road.
13.5 Cross intersection with Boston Post Road.
13.6 Continue straight at stop sign onto Old Kings Highway.

at this intersection instead and proceed 0.6 miles to the Tokeneke Elementary School at the corner of Old Farm Road and Tokeneke Road. There you can pick up Ride #17 from *Short Bike Rides in Connecticut* for a ride into neighboring Rowayton.]

About 0.5 miles along Locust Hill Road, watch for a **stone marker** at the beginning of Goodwives River Road on the left. The marker proclaims that George Washington passed the point on three different occasions between 1756 and 1779, on his way to Boston. Chances are he was not on a bicycle!

Goodwives River Road follows its namesake river closely, coming to an end as the river opens to Long Island Sound. Continue straight at the stop sign, marking the end of Goodwives River Road and the beginning of Pear Tree Point Road. Looping around the point, you will pass a boat-filled marina and, next door, **Pear Tree Point Beach.** The beach is a pleasant place to stop, rest, and cool off on a warm summer day and offers a great view of Long Island.

Completing the Pear Tree Point loop on Long Neck Point Road, proceed to the left across a picturesque stone bridge over the Goodwives River. On the river's west bank is the **Webb House** (circa 1800) and **Rings End Landing.** Also known as Gorham's Landing, this was the site of one of Darien's earliest commercial centers, dating back to the early eighteenth century.

Rings End Road, an uphill run, brings you to the Boston Post Road (Route 1) and into the Noroton Heights section of Darien. Zigzag left onto Route 1, then right onto Noroton Avenue, and put on those climbing shoes once again, because it is a slow climb for the next 0.7 mile up to West Avenue. Thankfully, West Avenue is mostly level.

If you are getting a little hot about now, you will welcome the left turn onto Stony Brook Road. This heavily wooded lane can turn a sweltering afternoon into a cool, springlike day.

At the end of Stony Brook Road, the route circles along Leroy Avenue to Middlesex Avenue, and onto High School Lane. Up ahead is Darien High School. Take a shortcut through the school's campus to end up on Hollow Tree Ridge Road.

Now here is a road that was meant to be ridden! Hollow Tree Ridge Road will take you all the way to the New Canaan town line in style. Along the way you will pass the elegant Wee Burn Country Club, many equally elegant homes, and two stop signs—keep to the left both times and enjoy the ride.

A third stop sign marks the northern end of both Hollow Tree Ridge Road and Darien. On the right corner of this four-way intersection is the small, quaint Talmadge Hill Community Church.

Turn right onto Talmadge Hill Road and continue to its end. Then take a right onto Mansfield Avenue (Route 124) and a left two blocks later onto Stephen Mather Road. Be extremely careful when turning onto Mather; there's a blind curve just ahead. [If, however, you wish to join up with Ride #24, which loops through New Canaan, turn left at Mansfield Avenue for the 2-mile ride into that town's center.]

As you approach the corner of Mather and Brookside Road (where you will turn right), take a look at the colonial house on the left corner. This is the **Stephen Mather Homestead** (circa 1778), a National Historical Landmark. Mather is best remembered as the father of the United States National Park Service. Two other Mather family homes are found farther down Brookside.

The circuit concludes as Brookside Road crosses the Boston Post Road and merges into Kings Highway. Ahead lies the Goodwives Shopping Center and your journey's end.

For Further Information

Darien Historical Society (203) 655–9233

Getting There

The ride's starting point is easily accessible from Interstate 95 (Exit 12 northbound or exit 13 southbound) or the Merritt Parkway (Exit 37). From the Darien railroad station, cross the Boston Post Road onto Old Kings Highway and travel 0.3 miles to the Goodwives Shopping Center.

Fairfield County
New Canaan

Mileage:	9
Approximate pedaling time:	1.5 hours
Terrain:	Rolling; hilly in spots
Traffic:	Moderate in the center of town, light elsewhere
Things to see:	West Road colonial cemetery, New Canaan Nature Center, New Canaan Historical Society

The roads of northern New Canaan will challenge even the most seasoned cyclist. The flattest terrain is found along three north-south ridges, while east-west roads offer many ups and downs as they connect one ridge to the next. On this route you will enjoy some easier riding along all three ridges and face some truly challenging hills as you travel between them.

Leaving the center of New Canaan on Cherry Street, turn left onto Main Street as you follow the signs for Routes 124 north and 106 east. At the next intersection follow the ROUTE 106 EAST sign by turning right on East Avenue. Don't build up too much speed going down the short hill at the beginning of East, as you must turn left almost immediately onto Forest Avenue. Follow Forest until you come to an island in the middle of an intersection. Turn right, then left onto Smith Ridge Road (Route 123) heading north.

Smith Ridge is a pleasant road for cycling thanks to an abundant shoulder. As the road veers around to the left close to the crest of a fairly long hill, turn left onto Country Club Road. This is an appropriate name indeed, for the road travels along the southern edge of the New Canaan Country Club's golf course.

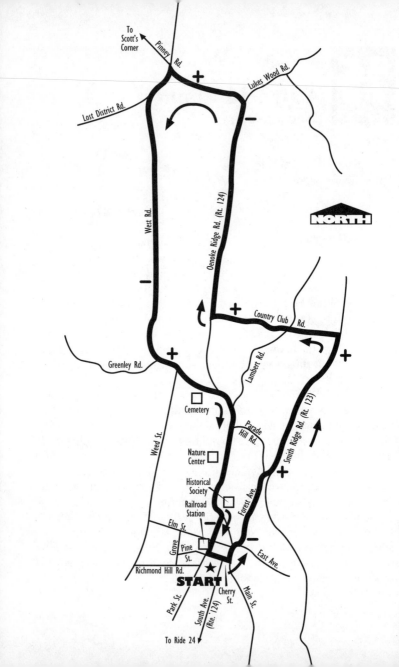

To Scott's Corner

Pinney Rd.

Lukes Wood Rd.

Lost District Rd.

West Rd.

Oenoke Ridge Rd. (Rt. 124)

NORTH

Country Club Rd.

Greenley Rd.

Lambert Rd.

Smith Ridge Rd. (Rt. 123)

Cemetery

Parade Hill Rd.

Weed St.

Nature Center

Historical Society

Forest Ave.

Railroad Station

Elm St.

Grove

Pine St.

East Ave.

Richmond Hill Rd.

★ START

Park St.

South Ave. (Rte. 124)

Cherry St.

Main St.

To Ride 24

DIREC-TIONS at a glance

0.0	Start at the intersection of South Avenue and Cherry Street; follow the signs toward Routes 124 north and 106 east.
0.1	Left onto Main Street.
0.2	Right onto East Avenue, then immediately left onto Forest Avenue.
0.6	Right, then immediately left onto Smith Ridge Road (Route 123 north).
1.8	Left onto Country Club Road.
2.7	Right onto Oenoke Ridge Road (Route 124 north).
4.2	Veer left to follow Route 124 at intersection with Lukes Woods Road. Route 124 changes names to Pinney Road.
4.8	Left onto West Road.
5.1	At stop sign, continue left on West Road.
7.5	At end of West Road, go straight to rejoin Oenoke Ridge Road (Route 124), this time heading south.
8.5	Sharp left (just before downhill) onto Park Street.
8.6	At stop sign, continue straight down hill on Park Street.
8.8	Left at second stop light onto Cherry Street.
8.9	The ride concludes at the intersection of Cherry and Main streets.

A few steep ups and downs later, turn to the right onto Oenoke Ridge Road (Route 124). Oenoke Ridge winds northward, alternating between shaded and open expanses. The views and scenery more than make up for the road's slow uphill slope. Keep an eye out for the New Canaan Reservoir, located below the ridge to the right along the road's long, open straightaway.

As Oenoke Ridge blends into Pinney Road around a sharp curve to the left, the terrain takes a marked turn downward toward a small bridge crossing the Rippowam River, only to be followed by an equally steep uphill run. Shortly after the hill's crest, turn left onto West Road for the return trip to New Canaan. [If all this climbing has been a bit much, and right now you want nothing more than a cold drink, continue past West Road for another mile or so. Crossing into Westchester County, New York, you will come upon a cyclist's oasis—Scotts Corners. There you will find all the amenities needed for a quick roadside refueling. Once rejuvenated, you may either pedal back up (sorry) to West Road or continue on Route 124 north into Pound Ridge. If you choose the latter, turning left onto Pound Ridge Road will take you into Bedford, where Ride #15 commences.]

West Road is heavily shaded and largely downhill—just what the doctor ordered! Traveling southward, sharp-eyed cyclists will spot a small **colonial cemetery** on the right just before the intersection with Oenoke Ridge Road. Cordoned off by a wooden picket fence, the cemetery grounds are marked by a small sign that proclaims this as the first site of the Church of England in New Canaan, dating back to May 13, 1764.

Continue along Oenoke Ridge Road (Route 124) to the south. You will soon come upon the **New Canaan Nature Center** on your right. The center features hiking trails, a visitors' center, a greenhouse, a maple syrup shed, an Audubon House, and a cider mill. The immaculate grounds and trails are open daily from dawn to dusk, while the buildings are open Tuesday through Sunday. Admission is free.

As you once again approach the center of New Canaan, Oenoke Ridge Road takes a sharp turn to the left. This is your cue to prepare for an equally sharp right turn onto Park Street. Park passes between the town's green and the New Canaan Congregational Church. Across Oenoke Ridge Road from this sharp turn is the home of the **New Canaan Historical Society**. If time permits, you might want to tour their facilities.

Continue down Park, turning to the left at the second traffic light onto Cherry Street. Follow Cherry for one block to the corner of South Avenue, the ride's starting point. [If you wish, turn right onto South (Route 124) and continue for 2 miles across the town line. There you may join our tour of Darien (Ride #24) at the corner of Talmadge Hill Road and Mansfield Avenue.]

For Further Information

New Canaan Historical Society (203) 966–1776
New Canaan Nature Center (203) 966–9577

Getting There

New Canaan is most easily reached from Exit 37 on the Merritt Parkway (Route 15). Bear left on the off ramp to head north on Route 124 into the center of town. For mass-transit service, take the Metro North railroad (New Haven line), transferring to the New Canaan branch in Stamford. As you leave the station, turn right onto Park Street and then left at Cherry.

Fairfield County
Westport

Mileage:	19
Approximate pedaling time:	3 hours
Terrain:	Rolling
Traffic:	Moderate near Sherwood Island State Park on summer weekends, light elsewhere
Things to see:	Nature Center for Environmental Activities, Rolnick Observatory, Sherwood Island State Park

If you are a fan of the old "I Love Lucy" television show, then you surely remember when the Ricardos moved from New York City to the country. There, Lucy was pitted against rural life, complete with livestock and a farmhouse. "The country," as they identified it, was Westport, Connecticut. And while few Westporters till the soil for a living today, many of the town's roads continue to offer rural charm, as you are about to discover.

Begin the ride from the north side of the Westport railroad station, located off Park Street in the Saugatuck section of town. Head north on Riverside Avenue, which is appropriately named, as it follows along the western shore of the Saugatuck River. The river opens into Long Island Sound after starting high in the hills of northern Fairfield County.

About 1 mile later turn left onto Sylvan Road. As it intersects Riverside Avenue, Sylvan divides into two one-way lanes separated by an automotive service station. Turn left *after* the service station to follow the flow of traffic.

NORTH

Stony Brook Rd.

Nature Center

Old Hill Rd.

Wilton Rd. (Rte. 33)

Weston Rd. (Rte. 57)

Easton Rd. (Rte. 136)

Merritt Parkway (Route 15)

Cross Highway

Rolnick Observatory

Woodside Ln.

Main St.

Sylvan Rd.

Kings Hwy.

Canal St.

Main St.

Compo Road North

Bayberry Ln.

Riverside Ave.

Saugatuck River

Boston Post Rd. (Rte. 1)

Long Lots Rd.

START

Bridge St.

Compo Rd. South

Greens Farms Rd.

Sherwood Island Connector

Turkey Hill Rd.

Minuteman Statue

Compo Rd. South

Hills Point Rd.

Clapboard Hill Rd.

Compo Beach

Sherwood Island State Park

Connecticut Turnpike (I–95)

LONG ISLAND SOUND

DIREC-TIONS at a glance

0.0   From the Westport railroad station head north on Riverside Avenue.

0.3   Right at traffic light to continue on Riverside Avenue.

1.0   Left onto Sylvan Road.

2.0   Right onto Stony Brook Road.

2.3   Left onto Woodside Lane.

2.5   Right into Nature Center for Environmental Activities. Return the same way you entered.

2.9   Left onto Stony Brook Road.

3.2   Right onto unmarked Old Hill Road.

3.5   Left onto Kings Highway North.

4.2   Left onto Canal Street (Route 57), which soon becomes Main Street.

5.0   Straight as Main Street changes to Easton Road (Route 136).

6.9   Right onto Bayberry Lane.

9.7   Right onto Long Lots Road.

10.3 Left onto Turkey Hill Road.

11.5 Right onto Clapboard Hill Road.

12.1 Right onto Greens Farms Road.

12.4 Left onto Sherwood Island Connector.

13.1 Enter Sherwood Island State Park.

13.6 Exit Sherwood Island State Park.

14.3 Left onto Greens Farms Road.

15.2 Left onto Hills Point Road.

16.3 Follow the road to the right as it changes names to Compo Road South.

18.1 Left onto Bridge Street (Route 136).

18.7 Left onto Riverside Avenue.

19.0 Back at Westport railroad station.

Climbing upward on Sylvan, travel across the Boston Post Road (Route 1). Though the climb may seem as though it will last forever, the route suddenly veers sharply downward and to the right as it joins Stony Brook Road. At the bottom of the hill turn left at the four-way intersection with Woodside Lane.

At the end of Woodside on the right is the entrance to the **Nature Center for Environmental Activities.** Open from 9 A.M. to 5 P.M. Monday through Saturday and 1 to 4 P.M. on Sundays, the center is a sixty-two-acre wildlife refuge complete with a visitors' hall and a well-groomed set of hiking trails. Inside the building you will find exhibits of plants and animals and displays of fossils and minerals, as well as terrariums and aquariums. A nominal donation is requested upon entering.

Return down Woodside Lane and bear left at the four-way stop back onto Stony Brook Road. At its end turn right onto unmarked Old Hill Road and then left onto Kings Highway North. Kings Highway is famous for being the first colonial "highway," connecting towns between New York City and Boston.

After Kings Highway crosses the Saugatuck River, veer left onto Canal Street. Canal soon blends into Main Street. [If you wish to shorten the ride, turn right in about 0.5 mile onto North Clinton Avenue (Route 136 south) as it intersects Main Street. Doing so will bring you back to the railroad station in 3 miles.]

If you are sticking with the ride for the long haul, stay on Route 136 north (Easton Road). A rather confusing intersection lies another 0.3 mile down the road. As Route 57 (now called Weston Road) breaks off to the left, continue straight on Easton Road. Crossing under the Merritt Parkway, Easton Road continues on a perfectly straight (albeit slightly uphill) trajectory past the elegant wooded residences of northeastern Westport.

About 2 miles after the split from Route 57, turn right onto Bayberry Lane. Bayberry begins with a curvy, uphill run but eventually flattens out. Just after crossing under the Merritt Parkway again, take a look on your left for a sign pointing to **Rolnick Observatory.** The observatory site is remembered by locals as a 1950s' U.S. Army installation used to track Nike missiles. The site was deeded to the local school district a decade later, and an observatory was built atop a 40-foot-high tower found well beyond the road, behind three barracks-style buildings. Today the Rolnick Observatory houses a fine telescope that is operated and maintained by volunteers from the Westport Astronomical Society. The observatory is open for public viewing on clear Wednesday and Thursday evenings from 8 to 10 P.M.

Stay on Bayberry all the way to its end at Long Lots Road. Turn right onto Long Lots; in 0.6 mile take a left onto Turkey Hill Road. From Turkey Hill turn right onto Clapboard Hill Road and right again onto Greens Farms Road. Along the way you will pass some of the town's few remaining pastures.

Turn left at the four-way intersection with the multilane Sherwood Island Connector, following it over Interstate 95 and into **Sherwood Island State Park**. Care *must* be exercised on the connector, especially when passing the entrance ramp leading to the interstate, as cars have a habit of going a little too fast here.

Once inside Sherwood Island State Park, the pace slows down to a more peaceful level. The park roads offer a serene tour of the facilities, which include picnic areas, bathing beaches, and a great view of Long Island. In the spring it is especially nice to pull under the shade of a tree and watch all the kites being flown.

Exit the park along the connector, turning left in 0.7 mile to continue along Greens Farms Road. At the next major intersection turn left onto Hills Point Road. Hills Point will take you back toward Long Island Sound and Compo Beach. Rounding a bend along the shore, the road changes names to Compo Road South. At the intersection with Compo Beach Road watch for a statue of a Revolutionary War Minuteman in the middle of the road. A sign on the statue's pedestal reads TO COMMEMORATE THE HEROISM OF THE PATRIOTS WHO DEFENDED THEIR COUNTRY WHEN THE BRITISH INVADED THE STATE, APRIL 25, 1777.... The Minuteman has been standing watch here since 1906.

Continue along Compo Road, crossing under the Connecticut Turnpike (Interstate 95) and turning left onto Bridge Street (Route 136). Follow Bridge Street to its end on the other side of the Saugatuck River. The ride concludes with a left onto Riverside Avenue back to the railroad station parking lot.

For Further Information

Nature Center for Environmental Activities (203) 227–7253
Rolnick Observatory (203) 227–0925
Sherwood Island State Park (203) 226–6983

Getting There

The Westport railroad station is easily accessible from the Connecticut Turnpike (Interstate 95). Northbound traffic should exit at Exit 17, continue straight across Saugatuck Avenue onto Park Street, and bear right at the end into the parking lot. Southbound drivers should also exit at Exit 17, turning right onto Saugatuck Avenue, then left onto Park. Metro North makes frequent stops at Westport throughout the day for those who wish to journey there by train.

Essex County
Livingston to West Orange

Mileage:	20
Approximate pedaling time:	3 hours
Terrain:	Hilly
Traffic:	Moderate
Things to see:	Eagle Rock Reservation, Edison National Historical Site, South Mountain Reservation, Turtle Back Zoo (optional)

The Livingston-West Orange Loop has all the ingredients of a challenging, diverse ride. There are dramatic climbs and sensational descents. Along the way you will experience a wide variety of traffic conditions—from city congestion to rural isolation—within just a few miles.

From the center of Livingston, head east on Mount Pleasant Avenue (Route 10). Though traffic can be heavy, the road's shoulder allows for a placid coexistence between "them" and "us." After climbing a hill turn left onto Laurel Avenue, a tranquil thoroughfare lined with attractive homes. The road's only drawback is the poor quality of the shoulder after the road crosses over Interstate 280.

Laurel Avenue ends at the Crestmount Country Club and Eagle Rock Avenue, where the route turns right. The beautifully manicured lawn of the golf course provides a little solace as the road climbs up and up and up.

When you reach the peak bear left into **Eagle Rock Reservation.** If you didn't lose your breath on the climb to the park, you will once you see the view! To the east is a magnificent panorama of New York City. You'll see the Empire State Building, the World Trade Center,

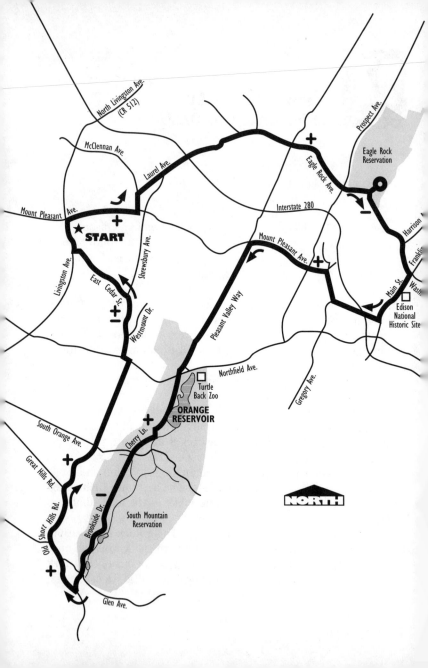

DIRECTIONS at a glance

0.0	Begin at the corner of Livingston Avenue and Mount Pleasant Road (Route 10). Proceed east on Mount Pleasant.
0.9	Left onto Laurel Avenue.
1.1	Right to stay on Laurel Avenue.
2.7	Right onto Eagle Rock Avenue.
5.3	Left into Eagle Rock Reservation.
6.1	Right onto Main Street.
7.3	Right onto Mount Pleasant Avenue (Route 10).
9.3	Left onto Pleasant Valley Way.
14.5	Right onto Old Short Hills Road.
17.9	Left onto Northfield Avenue.
18.0	Right onto East Cedar Street.
18.7	Left to stay on East Cedar Street.
19.7	Right onto Livingston Avenue.

and many other skyscrapers. You can also see the Bayonne and Goethals bridges connecting New Jersey with Staten Island as well as the towers of the Verrazano-Narrows Bridge, which links Staten Island and Brooklyn. If you're hungry, you can enjoy the view from the High Lawn Pavilion, a huge, very pink building that offers the finest in "scenic dining."

Exiting the reservation, carefully proceed to the left on Eagle Rock Avenue. The road plummets downhill, but avoid building up too much speed because at the bottom the route turns right onto Main Street. Welcome to West Orange.

About a mile along Main Street, watch for signs to the **Edison National Historical Site**. A three-story brick factory, this was Edison's largest and last workplace. It was here that Edison and a staff of sixty co-workers devised more than half of his 1,093 patents. Now run by the National Parks Service, the building is open daily from 9 A.M. to 1 P.M. and offers tours, exhibits, and presentations. A modest entrance fee is charged for adults, but children are free.

Turn right onto Mount Pleasant Avenue (Route 10) to leave downtown West Orange. In 2 miles the route turns left onto Pleasant Valley Way. (If you want a shortcut, continue straight for 2.5 miles back to Livingston.)

After crossing Northfield Avenue the road changes names to Cherry Lane and enters **South Mountain Reservation**, a delightful nature preserve. The reservation's north entrance is highlighted by Orange Reservoir on the left and large open fields on the right. (For a quick side trip, turn left onto Northfield. Just down the road is the **Turtle Back Zoo**.)

Crossing South Orange Avenue, the road changes its name to Brookside Drive. Not far beyond, watch through the trees for an old factory on the left. Though it may look out of place among the natural surroundings, the factory apparently once made use of the stream that has followed the road since the reservoir.

As the reservation ends turn right onto Old Short Hills Road. The hills may be old but they are anything but short as the road rises back toward Livingston. Zigzag onto Northfield Avenue and then onto East Cedar Street for the final leg of the ride. East Cedar is a real roller coaster of a road. Keep an eye out at the bottom of a hill for a faded green-and-white sign indicating that East Cedar continues to the left. (Missing the turn puts you on Shrewsbury Avenue, an *up*lifting experience that you do not need.) Turn right on Livingston Avenue for the short skip back into town.

For Further Information

Eagle Rock Reservation (201) 731–3000
Edison National Historic Site (201) 736–5050
South Mountain Reservation (201) 731–5800

Getting There

The Livingston area is most easily accessible by taking the North Livingston Avenue (County Route 512) exit off Interstate 280. Head south for 1.6 miles into the center of Livingston, where you will find ample parking along the roads or in shopping-center parking lots.

Passaic County
Greenwood Lake

Mileage:	19
Approximate pedaling time:	3 hours
Terrain:	Hilly
Traffic:	Light
Things to see:	Greenwood Lake, Wanaque Wildlife Area

Bridging the border between Passaic County, New Jersey, and Orange County, New York, is a favorite getaway for residents of both states. Nestled in a protective valley, **Greenwood Lake** is a beautiful natural resource whose encircling roads provide spectacular views of both the water and the surrounding hills.

Speaking of hills, this ride has a few beauties! When choosing the route we had a difficult time deciding on the direction of travel—clockwise or counterclockwise—around the lake. We finally settled on clockwise, but you may prefer the reverse. Either way, the route challenges a rider's stamina.

Begin at the ShopRite Shopping Center, which is wedged between Union Valley Road (County Route 513) and Marshall Hill Road in West Milford. There are stores galore here in case you need some last-minute supplies. From here head north on Union Valley. In about 0.25 mile watch for picturesque Pinecliff Lake through the trees on the left.

The ride continues to the right onto Warwick Turnpike, followed by a left onto Lakeside Road (County Route 511). Although Lakeside is unmarked, it is easy to find thanks to an Exxon gas station and "Bill's Automotive Service Center" on its corners. And the road certainly does live up to its invisible name as it journeys along the west

DIREC-TIONS at a glance

0.0	Head north on Union Valley Road (County Route 513).
1.3	Right at sign for Greenwood Lake to stay on Union Valley Road.
1.6	Right onto Warwick Turnpike.
2.0	Left onto unmarked Lakeside Road (County Route 511).
8.0	Straight on Church Street.
8.2	Left at stop sign onto Grove Avenue.
8.3	Right at stop sign onto Waterstone Road.
8.4	Right onto Sterling Forest Road.
15.9	Right onto Greenwood Lake Turnpike (County Route 511).
17.5	Left onto Marshall Hill Road.
18.3	Left to stay on Marshall Hill Road.
18.8	Back at ShopRite shopping center.

shore of Greenwood Lake. The view just keeps getting better as you pedal northward, but so do the hills as the road skirts the eastern face of Bearfort Mountain and Hewitt State Forest. Although Lakeside remains hilly for its entire length, it becomes wider and offers a better shoulder once it crosses into New York State. At the same time, the designation changes to Route 210.

Approaching the village of Greenwood Lake, Route 210 turns off to the left, but our ride proceeds straight on Church Street. Before continuing, however, you may wish to follow Route 210 into the village itself, where there is a nice deli and a fragrant bakery.

Exit the village of Greenwood Lake by following Church Street to unmarked Grove Avenue and Waterstone Road (also sans street sign). Finally, turn right onto Sterling Forest Road after crossing a small bridge over the lake. The road starts out on the bumpy and narrow side but will become smoother as it heads south. Not far out of town is a small park on the right that makes a nice place for a roadside picnic.

Sterling Forest Road is an exciting route to cycle. Though peppered with hills, much of the road scoots right along the water's edge.

Cyclists not only see Greenwood Lake, they *experience* it on Sterling Forest Road! Just try not to get so carried away with the view that you ride off the road into the lake itself!

Crossing back into New Jersey, Sterling Forest Road changes names to East Shore Road, thankfully becoming wider and smoother in the transition. Still following the lake on the right, the road is now accompanied by the **Wanaque Wildlife Area** on the left, although it is unmarked and has no obvious public entrance. Shortly, as East Shore Road turns away from the lake, a stream joins in on the left. This is the Wanaque River, which features several small cascades and miniature falls as it descends along with the road.

East Shore Road ends at a large triangular island, where our route turns right onto Greenwood Lake Turnpike (County Route 511). [If you wish, you may join Ride #2 from *Short Bike Rides in New Jersey* by turning left here.] Ever climbing, proceed left onto Marshall Hill Road as County Route 511 veers to the right. If you need a little extra "oomph" to make it the rest of the way, you can choose from either an A&W root beer stand at this intersection or a Dairy Queen ice cream stand farther up Marshall Hill. Thankfully, Marshall Hill is the last big climb back into West Milford and the shopping center from where you began.

For Further Information

Greenwood Lake (201) 728–8505

Getting There

West Milford can be reached by taking Exit 37 off Interstate 80, then following County Route 513 north; or by taking Exit 15 (Suffern) off the New York State Thruway (Interstate 87), then following Route 17 north to Route 72 west and finally County Route 511 west to County Route 513 into town.

Morris/Sussex Counties
Lake Hopatcong

Mileage:	16
Approximate pedaling time:	2.5 hours
Terrain:	Hilly
Traffic:	Light to moderate
Things to see:	Lake Hopatcong, Hopatcong State Park

Northwestern New Jersey, nicknamed the Skylands, offers some of the finest (and hilliest) cycling terrain in the tristate region. Dominating the area is the state's largest body of water, **Lake Hopatcong.** Actually, when Europeans first settled the area in the early 1700s, they found here not one, but rather two, bodies of water. The smaller, northern lake was christened Little Pond, while the larger was named Great Pond or Brooklyn Pond. They were connected by the Musconetcong River.

With the discovery of iron ore in the 1750s, the region quickly developed a strong mining industry. The Brooklyn Forge, built along the Musconetcong between the lakes, supplied Washington's troops stationed in Moorestown during the American Revolution.

As the mining industry began to ebb because of the high cost of shipping the ore, the forge was dismantled and replaced by a dam. Completed in 1827, the dam raised the water in the river valley to form one large lake. The newly formed lake was named Hopatcong, from the Indian word *Huppakong,* meaning "honey waters of many coves."

Subsequently, a canal was built to link the lake with Easton, Pennsylvania, to the west and Jersey City, New Jersey, to the east. It took five days for mule-drawn barges to make the trip; they were soon re-

NORTH

Northwood Rd.

CR 609

Prospect Point Rd.

Bowling Green Pkwy.

Brady Rd.

Edison Rd.

Lakeside Ave.

Espanong Rd.

CR 609

Raccoon Island

Halsey Island

Minnisink Rd.

Southard Rd.

BEAR POND

Maxim Dr.

LAKE HOPATCONG

Berkshire Rd.

Maxim Dr.

CR 607

River Styx Rd.

Altenbrand Ave.

Howard Blvd.

Lakeside Blvd.

Chincopee Ave.

CR 607

Windemere Ave.

Hopatchung Rd.

Lakeside Blvd.

CR 607

Hopatcong State Park

Brooklyn Rd.

Mt. Arlington Blvd.

Center St.

★ START

Kings Hwy.

Landing Rd.

Shippenport Rd.

DIRECTIONS at a glance

0.0	Head east on Lakeside Boulevard from Grand Union Shopping Center.
0.4	Left at traffic light onto unmarked Shippenport Road.
0.5	Left onto Mount Arlington Boulevard.
2.8	Follow road toward the right onto Altenbrand Avenue.
3.0	Left onto Howard Boulevard.
5.8	Left onto Brady Road.
7.5	Left onto Northwood Road (County Route 609).
10.3	Left onto Maxim Drive (County Route 607).
13.6	Left at stop sign onto Hopatchung Road.
13.8	Right onto Lakeside Boulevard.
15.7	Right into shopping center.

placed by the locomotive. The canal was abandoned, and the lake returned to its natural serenity.

On this ride, you will experience firsthand the serenity of Lake Hopatcong while encountering the challenges of Morris and Sussex counties' countryside. Begin at the Grand Union Shopping Center at the corner of Lakeside Boulevard and Center Street in Landing. Though it is always a good idea to bring from home everything you will need on a ride, it's nice to know that the shopping center features a grocery store, a deli, and a bike shop . . . just in case!

With your needs and those of your trusty steed now satisfied, push eastward on Lakeside. Just down the road, after catching your first glimpse of the lake, turn left at the traffic light onto unmarked Shippenport Road. A second left on Mount Arlington Boulevard aims you northward along the east shore of Hopatcong. Though the road starts out bumpy and narrow, it improves in about a mile as it crosses into Mount Arlington. All along, watch as the houses on the left begin to sink below the grade of the road. The steeply inclined bank affords you a good view of their roofs and an even better glimpse of the water.

Follow the road to the right as it veers into Altenbrand Avenue. Just ahead a left at the stop sign puts you on Howard Boulevard. Enjoy the brief downhill respite as Howard dives toward the lake's Van Every Cove, where you will find a marina, boat rentals, and another great lakeside panorama.

After pedaling up and over another rise you will come to the town of Espanong and Great Cove. Passing another marina, the road ascends again on its way northward. A few more ups and downs later, turn left onto Brady Road. It would be very easy to ride right by this turn without ever noticing it, were it not for the sign—not the street sign but the sign across the way advertising CHABON'S BAR. You can't miss it.

Brady Road begins with a flat stretch until it crosses Brady Bridge; then it's upward once again. As the hill tops out at Schwarz Road, Brady changes names to Prospect Point Road. Incidentally, you may think you have wandered into Washington, D.C., after the bridge, as you cycle past avenues with states' names.

Turn left onto Northwood Road (County Route 609) and cross into Sussex County. Bordered by few houses, Northwood winds through thick woodlands, up some hills, and down others and is a great road for cycling. As it ends at Maxim Drive (County Route 607) you can sneak a peek at Bear Pond on the right if you want, but the ride proceeds along River Styx Road to the left for the (mostly) downhill trip through the borough of Hopatcong. Continue across the bridge over River Styx to the road's end at a stop sign. Turn left onto Hopatchung Road, then right up ahead onto Lakeside Boulevard.

For the final leg of the journey, Lakeside Boulevard obliges with a downhill profile. Close to the bottom of the hill lies **Hopatcong State Park** on the left. A small admission fee is charged. The park features a swimming beach, picnic area, fishing, and a refreshment stand. A museum, run by the local historical society, is open to visitors daily from 1 P.M. to 4 P.M. Why not ride the half mile back to the shopping center, pick up some food, and return to the park for an end-of-ride picnic? Go ahead, you deserve it!

For Further Information

Lake Hopatcong (201) 770–1200
Hopatcong State Park (201) 398–7010

Getting There

The starting point in Landing can be reached from Exit 28 North off Interstate 80. Follow the signs toward Hopatcong State Park on Lakeside Boulevard. The shopping center is on the left, about 0.5 mile before the park.

BOROUGH OF

Harrington Park

FOUNDED 1904

PLANTINGS
BY
HARRINGTON PARK
WOMAN'S CLUB

Bergen County
Harrington Park and Vicinity

Mileage:	14
Approximate pedaling time:	2 hours
Terrain:	Mostly flat
Traffic:	Light to moderate
Things to see:	Abram Demaree Homestead, Oradell Reservoir, Lafayette marker, Pascack Brook County Park, Baylor's Massacre site, Lake Tappan, Pondside Park

We have always liked this town in northern Bergen County, New Jersey. Its name has such a pleasant ring to it! (Of course, we Harringtons might be a little biased in its favor.) On this ride you will pass through Harrington Park as well as a number of other "bedroom communities" to New York City.

Begin at the corner of Tappan Road and Schraalenburgh Road, heading south on the latter. Ahead, be sure to stay to the right as Closter Road forks to the left. Shortly, at the edge of town, Schraalenburgh passes over a small stream called Dwarskill.

On the right corner of the intersection of Old Hook Road, take a few minutes to visit the **Abram Demaree Homestead.** Demaree, a farmer from Holland, purchased the house, barn, and adjacent land here in 1769. (The house dates back to 1720; the barn to the late 1600s.) Today Demaree's home has been transformed into an old-fashioned country store featuring more than one million crafts, gifts, and seasonal decorations. Hours vary by season, so be sure to phone ahead.

Continue down Schraalenburgh until the junction with Durie Avenue, where the ride turns right. A little ways down the road, just be-

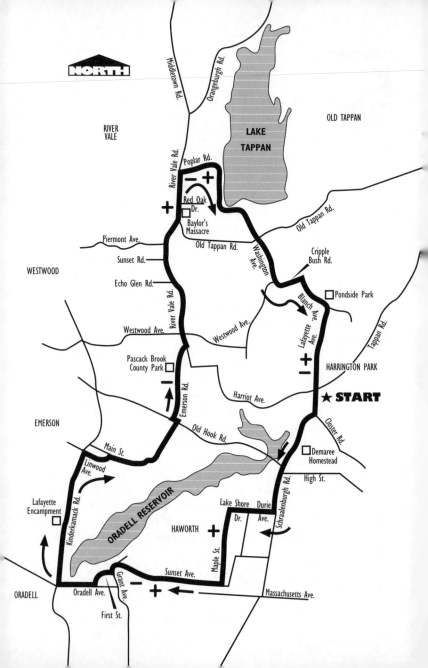

DIREC-TIONS at a glance

0.0	Begin at Tappan Road-Schraalenburgh Road intersection.
0.2	Right to stay on Schraalenburgh Road.
1.4	Right onto Durie Avenue.
1.5	Straight onto Lake Shore Drive.
1.9	Left onto Maple Street.
2.7	Right onto Sunset Avenue.
4.0	Left onto Grant Avenue.
4.2	Right onto First Street.
4.5	Right onto Oradell Avenue.
4.9	Right onto Kinderkamack Road (County Route 51).
6.4	Right onto Linwood Avenue (merges ahead into Main Street).
7.9	Left onto Old Hook Road.
8.0	Right onto Emerson Road.
8.7	Left onto River Vale Road.
10.1	Left to stay on River Vale Road.
10.8	Right onto Poplar Road.
12.2	Straight across Old Tappan Road onto Washington Avenue.
12.7	Follow road to left onto Cripple Bush Road.
13.1	Right onto Blanch Avenue.
13.5	Right onto Lafayette Road.
14.5	Back at starting point.

fore the railroad crossing, Durie shoots off to the left, but you should continue straight onto Lake Shore Drive. Not far down Lake Shore, a sign suddenly proclaims that the road ends ahead, forcing you to take a left onto Maple Street. Now in the town of Haworth, the ride along Maple leads through a lovely, shady neighborhood of pleasant homes.

Maple ends at the juncture with Sunset Avenue. A right turn here takes you on a course straight toward White Beeches Country Club and **Oradell Reservoir.** In fact, the road slices through the club's property, affording a good view of the well-manicured golf course.

At the end of Sunset Avenue, with the reservoir dead ahead, keep to the left as the road becomes Grant Avenue. Follow the green-and-white BIKE ROUTE signs to the right onto First Street for a quick jaunt through another quiet neighborhood.

At the street's end turn right onto Oradell Avenue for the trip into its namesake village. Just after crossing the Oradell Veterans Memorial Bridge over the tip of the reservoir, you will pass a small park on the right. A stone marker in the center proclaims this to be a memorial to veterans of World War I.

Turn right onto Kinderkamack Road (County Route 51). Kinderkamack can be a busy thoroughfare at times, so ride with caution. Be especially wary of cars parked along the road whose drivers suddenly open their doors into traffic.

About 0.5 mile later, on the left-hand side of Kinderkamack, is a historical **marker** situated in front of a high ridge. The sign notes that for about two weeks in September 1778, the French general Lafayette chose this ridge as a campsite for the Continental Army. Today the army tents of two centuries ago have been replaced by three contemporary homes.

Just after crossing the railroad tracks at the Emerson train station, turn right on Linwood Avenue and continue onto Main Street. When Main Street ends at Old Hook Road, take a left followed by an immediate right onto Emerson Road. Before the road crosses into the town of River Vale, you will pass **Pascack Brook County Park** on the left. This is a great place to pull over for a midride reprieve.

At the next major intersection, turn left onto River Vale Road. As you approach Echo Glen Road on the left, a bike-route sign points to the start of a paved bicycle path, also on the left. Though the path is wonderful while it lasts, it ends in about 0.5 mile at Sunset Road.

As Old Tappan Road joins in from the right, a brown-and-white sign straight ahead marks the site of **Baylor's Massacre**. Take a quick right on Red Oak Drive to enter the commemorative park. The sign there reads: IN MEMORIAL OF AMERICAN SOLDIERS KILLED DURING THE REVOLUTIONARY WAR IN THE BAYLOR MASSACRE ON SEPTEMBER 28, 1778. LIEUTENANT COLONEL GEORGE BAYLOR'S THIRD REGIMENT OF CONTINENTAL DRAGOONS TOOK QUARTERS FOR THE NIGHT AT SEVERAL NEARBY FARMS. TORIES BETRAYED THEIR PRESENCE TO A BRITISH FORCE, WHO SURROUNDED THE

DRAGOONS DURING THE NIGHT. A NUMBER OF AMERICANS WERE KILLED OR WOUNDED AFTER THEY HAD SURRENDERED. The park features paved footpaths that wander through the woods toward the Hackensack River.

Turn right onto Poplar Road and enjoy a brief downhill run. But, remembering one of our laws of bicycling ("whatever goes down must go up"), get ready to pedal back up toward the shore of **Lake Tappan**. What a lovely ride this is along the lake's southwest shore! The view is especially breathtaking during autumn. You will soon cross a small bridge adjacent to the dam that regulates the water's depth. The prominent green pipe spanning the dam's width seems to be a favorite hangout for the local seagulls!

Leaving the lake behind, the road changes names to Washington Avenue. Continue across Old Tappan Road, veering to the left at its end onto Cripple Bush Road. A short while later take a right on Blanch Avenue, where a sign welcomes you back into Harrington Park. Although the ride turns right onto Lafayette Street, you may first elect to stop at **Pondside Park** on the left. The park, which features benches and a popular playground, is dedicated to the town's volunteers who "enrich Harrington Park life." Then it's a short trip down Lafayette to reach the ride's point of departure.

For Further Information

Abram Demaree Homestead (201) 784–9618

Getting There

Take Exit 2 off the Palisades Interstate Parkway. Turn left onto Route 9W, then right onto County Route 502 (Closter Dock Road). Stay on County Route 502 through the town of Closter, then turn right onto Knickerbocker Road (County Route 505). Follow the signs into Harrington Park.

Bicycling Clubs

National

Bikecentennial
P. O. Box 8308
Missoula, MO 59807

League of American Wheelmen
190 West Ostende Street
Suite 120
Baltimore, MD 21230

New York

American Youth Hostels
New York Council
891 Amsterdam Avenue
New York, NY 10025

Concerned Long Island
  Mountain Bikers
P. O. Box 203
Woodbury, NY 11797

Country Cycle Club, Inc.
1 Willowbrook Road
White Plains, NY 10605

Huntington Bicycle Club
P. O. Box 322
Huntington Station, NY 11746

Long Island Bicycle Club
P. O. Box 4493
Great Neck, NY 11023

Massapequa Park Bicycle Club
P. O. Box 231
Massapequa, NY 11758

Mid-Hudson Bicycle Club
P. O. Box 1727
Poughkeepsie, NY 12601

New York Cycle Club
P. O. Box 199
Cooper Station
New York, NY 10276

Orange County Bicycle Club
c/o Glen Van Cura
48 South Street
Goshen, NY 10924

Paumonok Bicycle Clubs, Inc.
P. O. Box 7159A
Hicksville, NY 11802

Staten Island Bicycling Club
P. O. Box 141016
Staten Island, NY 10314

Suffolk Bike Riders Association
P. O. Box 983
Hauppauge, NY 11788

Transportation Alternatives
494 Broadway
New York, NY 10012

Connecticut

Central Connecticut Cycling
c/o Dan Thurston
27 Lillian Drive
Trumbull, CT 06611

Hat City Cyclists
c/o Frank Malinowski
11 Elm Street, #2
Norwalk, CT 06850

Sound Cyclists Bicycle Club
c/o Roberta Davis
66 Overlook Road
Fairfield, CT 06430

New Jersey

Bicycle Touring Club of New Jersey
c/o Judi Burten
28 Wedgewood Drive, #42
Verona, NJ 07044

Central Jersey Bicycle Club
P. O. Box 2202
Edison, NJ 08818

Jersey Shore Touring Society
c/o Brian Schmult
P. O. Box 8581
Red Bank, NJ 07701

Morris Area Freewheelers
P. O. Box 331
Lake Hiawatha, NJ 07034

Outdoor Club of New Jersey
P. O. Box 1508
Riverside, NJ 08075

Princeton Freewheelers, Inc.
P. O. Box 1204
Princeton, NJ 08542

Shore Cycle Club
P. O. Box 492
Northfield, NJ 08225

Sussex County Touring Club
c/o Louis Lederhaas
17 North Orchard Terrace
Sparta, NJ 07871

Western Jersey Wheelmen
c/o Robert Boysen
P. O. Box 230-B, Philhower Road
Lebanon, NJ 08833

Annual Cycling Events

New York

   Bike-Boat-Bike Ride, sponsored by Suffolk Bike Riders Association
   Five Borough Bicycle Tour, sponsored by American Youth Hostels
      (canceled in 1991; will it return?)
   Golden Apple Century, sponsored by Country Cycle Club
   High Point Hundred, sponsored by Paumonok Bicycle Clubs
   New York City Century Ride-a-Thon, sponsored by
      Transportation Alternatives
   New York Ride across the State, sponsored by Mid-Hudson Bicycle Club

Connecticut

   Bloomin' Metric Century, sponsored by Sound Cyclists Bicycle Club

New Jersey

   Hillier Than Thou Century, sponsored by Central Jersey Bicycle Club
   Jersey Double, sponsored by Western Jersey Wheelmen
   New Jersey Farmlands Flat Tour, sponsored by Central Jersey
      Bicycle Club
   Pinelands Metric Century, sponsored by Shore Cycle Club
   Princeton Bicycling Event, sponsored by Princeton Freewheelers

Bicycle Shops and Rental Centers

Here is a brief list of some of the many fine bicycle shops and rental centers found in the tristate area. This list is by no means exhaustive, nor does it imply any endorsement by the authors or publisher.

Manhattan

Bicycle Habitat, 244 Lafayette Street. (212) 431–3315.
Canal Street Bicycles, 417 Canal Street. (212) 334–8000.
Citycycles, 659 Broadway. (212) 254–4457.
Frank's Bike Shop, 553 Grand Street. (212) 533–6332.
Gene's, 242 East 79th Street. (212) 249–9218.
Loeb Boathouse, East Park Drive, Central Park. (212) 288–7281.
West Side Bicycle Store, 231 West 96th Street. (212) 663–7531.

Brooklyn

Bay Ridge Bicycle World, 8916 3rd Avenue. (718) 238–1118.
Bicycle Land, 424 Coney Island Avenue. (718) 633–0820.
Brooklyn Bicycle Center, 717 Coney Island Avenue. (718) 941–9095.
Kings Highway Cycle, 728 Kings Highway. (718) 339–9830.
Larry's Cycle Shop, 1854 Flatbush Avenue. (718) 377–3600.
P & H Bicycle Store, 1819 Coney Island Avenue. (718) 998–4333.
Phil's Fixit Shop, 2308 86th Street. (718) 372–1013.
Pro Bike, 378 7th Avenue. (718) 965–2346.
Roy's Sheepshead Cycle, 2679 Coney Island Avenue. (718) 646–9430.
Sizzling Bicycle, Inc., 3100 Ocean Parkway. (718) 372–8985.
Trans-Bicycle, 2965 Ocean Avenue. (718) 743–2240.

Queens

Bayside Bicycle, Inc., 214-20 73rd Avenue, Bayside. (718) 776–5161.
Bicycle Place, 45-70 Kissena Boulevard, Flushing. (718) 358–0986.
Bicycles in Flushing Meadow Park, Flushing Meadow Park. (718) 669–9598.
Bikes Fantastique, 248-07 Union Turnpike, Bellrose. (718) 347–2726.
Buddy's Schwinn Bicycles, 79-30 Parsons Boulevard, Flushing.
    (718) 591–9180.
Master Cycle, Inc., 159-01 Northern Boulevard, Flushing. (718) 445–9118.
Roberts Bicycle, 33-13 Francis Lewis Boulevard, Bayside. (718) 353–5432.

Bronx

Arrow Cycle Inc., 4053 White Plains Road. (212) 547–2656.
Bronx Bike Center, 912 Gun Hill Road. (212) 798–3242.
Burke's Bicycle Shop, 941 Intervale Avenue. (212) 328–9197.
Castle Hill Bike Center, 1010 Castle Hill Avenue. (212) 597–2083.
Lezamas Bikes and Stuff, 312 East 167th Street. (212) 538–8352.
Sid's Bike Shop, 215 West 230th Street. (212) 549–8247.

Staten Island

Anthony's Bicycle Shop, 1203 Bay Street. (718) 981–5656.
Bennett's Bicycles, 517 Jewett Avenue. (718) 447–8652.
Bike Shop of Staten Island, 4026 Hylan Boulevard. (718) 948–4184.
Lombardi and Sons, 442 Bay Street. (718) 447–9722.
Roald Bike Shop, 1434 Richmond Road. (718) 351–7575.

Nassau County, New York

Bethpage Bicycle Shop, 355 Broadway, Bethpage. (516) 935–9688.
Bikeworks, 118 Glen Cove Road, East Hills. (516) 484–4422.
Brand's Cycle Center, 1966 Wantaugh Avenue, Wantaugh. (516) 781–6100.
Danny's Ride-a-Way, 3259 Hempstead Turnpike, Levittown.
    (516) 579–7770.
Sunrise Schwinn Cyclery, 4828 Sunrise Highway, Massapequa Park.
    (516) 798–5715.
Tony's Bike Shop, 3469 Merrick Road, Wantaugh. (516) 785–1669.

Suffolk County, New York

Babylon Bicycle Shop, 218 East Main Street, Babylon. (516) 587–6709.
Cycle Company, 564 Jericho Turnpike, Smithtown. (516) 979–7078.
Frenchy's Bike Shop, 1983 Union Boulevard, Bay Shore. (516) 665–6310.
Sally's Cycle, Inc., 213 Higbie Lane, West Islip. (516) 669–3174.
Smithtown Bicycle and Fitness Center, 11 West Main Street, Smithtown.
    (516) 265–5900.
South Bay Bicycle Shop, 179A Great East Neck Road, West Babylon.
    (516) 587–4143.

Westchester County, New York

Bicycle Express, 52 Virginia Road, North White Plains. (914) 428–2305.
Big Cycle, 9 Norm Avenue, Bedford Hills. (914) 666–3549.
Country Bike Center, 144 Bedford Road, Armonk. (914) 273–3454.
Cycling Centre of Westchester, 200 Hamilton Avenue, White Plains.
    (914) 682–4909.

Hickory and Tweed, 410 Main Street, Armonk. (914) 273–3397.
Miller's Bikes, 335 Mamaroneck Avenue, Mamaroneck. (914) 698–5070.
Rye Bike Shop, 30 Elm Place, Rye. (914) 967–2849.
Signature Cycles, Route 118, Somers. (914) 248–6311.

Putnam County, New York

Carmel Bicycle Shop, 7 Seminary Hill Road, Carmel. (914) 225–2599.
Lou's Bike Shop, Towners Road, Lake Carmel. (914) 225–3706.

Rockland County, New York

Congers Bike Shop, 104 Lake Road, Congers. (914) 268–3315.
Nyack Bicycle Outfitters, 72 North Broadway, Nyack. (914) 353–0268.
Valley Cycle, 8 East Route 59, Spring Valley. (914) 356–3179.

Orange County, New York

Bicycle Shop, Route 44, Pleasant Valley. (914) 635–3161.
Simons Cycle and Sport, 188 Main Street, Highland Falls. (914) 446–5252.
Vails Gate Cycle, Route 94, Vails Gate. (914) 565–7686.

Fairfield County, Connecticut

Buzz's Cycle Shop, Post Road, Old Greenwich. (203) 637–1665.
Greenwich Bicycles, 40 West Putnam Avenue, Greenwich. (203) 869–4141.
Jules Bicycle Shoppe, 876 Post Road, Darien. (203) 655–2300.
Pedal and Pump, 51 Tokeneke Road, Darien. (203) 655–2600.
Westport Bicycles, 1252 Post Road East, Westport. (203) 222–1998.

Bergen County, New Jersey

Albert's Westwood Cycle, 182 Third Avenue, Westwood. (201) 664–1688.
Paramus Cycle, 23 Farview Place, Paramus. (201) 368–8242.

Essex County, New Jersey

Cheapskates Bikes, 119 South Orange Avenue, South Orange.
    (201) 763–0277.
Northfield Cycle Company, 69 East Northfield Road, Livingston.
    (201) 992–6449.

Morris County, New Jersey

Bicycle Outlet, State Highway 15, Lake Hopatcong. (201) 663–1935.
Lakeside Cyclery, Lakeside Boulevard, Landing. (201) 398–7836.

Passaic County, New Jersey

Town Cycle, 1485 Union Valley Road, West Milford. (201) 728–8878.